IMPOSSIBILITIES BECOME CHALLENGES

By

Leonard W. Coote

A record of God's Faithfulness in saving, baptizing with the Holy Spirit, leading out into missionary work and supplying of daily needs.

Fifth Edition

A publication of

Church *Alive!* Press
8635 Callaghan Road
San Antonio, Texas 78230

Second Printing, fifth edition
January 1999

Impossibilities Become Challenges
Copyright © 1991, 1999
Church *Alive!* Press
All rights reserved.

All rights reserved. No part of this book may be reproduced in whole or in part without written permission from the author, except by a reviewer who may quote brief passages in a review; nor may any part of this book be reproduced, stored in a retrieval system, or transmitted in any form or by any means electronic, mechanical, including photocopying, record-ing, or other, without permission in writing from the author, except as provided by USA copyright law.

All Scripture quotations are from the *Holy Bible*, King James Version.

ISBN 1-892525-10-0

Printed in the United States of America

To obtain more copies please contact:
Church *Alive!* Press
8635 Callaghan Road
San Antonio, Texas 78230

ACKNOWLEDGMENTS

We wish to express our deepest appreciation to several people who voluntarily poured themselves out, giving their time and talents, for the completion of this fifth edition.

Several members of Revival Temple spent many hours typing the book into the computer. They were Gennie Barrera, John and Ruth Bell, Karen Eddleman, Barbara Estrada, Nathan Glasgow and Britt and Deanne White. We also want to thank Emily Adams, Hope Coote and Norma Trahan for their time and help with proof reading and editing.

Our appreciation also goes to Dave Bell for securing the appropriate publishing software and for spending many hours using his computer skills to format the pages for printing.

Working together to produce this edition was made more exciting by the many comments received from those who participated such as, "Now I can't wait to read the whole book!" or "What a blessing!" One person said, "I had been praying for a book that would do for me what this one has done! What an exciting life of total dedication to God! and what a challenge!"

FOREWORD

My first experience with Leonard Coote was at the Bible College I was attending in Tulsa, Oklahoma. I was interested in his daughter, Ruth, who was also a student. In fact, he was there to see her and, I think, to look me over also. I asked if I could have a talk with him and his reply was, "Let me have my afternoon nap first, then we will take a walk." I was young and had long legs but I had to quicken my steps to keep up with him.

Along the way he invited me to come to San Antonio to work with him. To prepare me he said, "Let me warn you, they call me a slave driver." I knew he meant that he was a hard worker and expected the same of others. I replied, "Brother Coote, I was raised on the farm and I am not afraid of hard work." After graduation I accepted his invitation and joined in the work he had begun in San Antonio.

A year later Ruth and I were married and served as his assistants. We were able to witness the development of the Emmanuel Church and International Bible College and to observe the methods of ministry of this great man of God. His vision drove him to long hours of hard work whether in the church, the Bible college or the work in Japan. It was from Brother Coote that I received a vision for missions and for class and excellence in ministry.

In 1954 I was invited for five weeks of ministry with him in Japan. As we had services every night in all kinds of places, I was able to observe first hand the tremendous ministry of Leonard Coote in Japan. Two years later Ruth and I, with our sons, found ourselves on our way to Japan to assist in the work.

This book could not have a more appropriate name - Impossibilities Become Challenges. As you read it you will laugh, you will cry, you will shout, and you will be amazed over and over again as Brother Coote tells his story. How a 21 year old Englishman spent his lifetime in the land of the Rising Sun - over 50 years of dedicated service to the Lord - makes an exciting narrative of the romance of missions. May this book enable you to challenge all impossibilities.

John M. Bell
San Antonio, Texas

PREFACE

It was in the late 1950's that I first learned of pastor and missionary Leonard W. Coote and his magnificent labor of love for his Lord and the Japanese people. As a student in grade school I found a friend who was Japanese. He with his family moved to the United States in the early 1920's. Nobuyuki Koyama and I became fast friends and for six years were inseparable. Then he and his family returned to Japan. Out of that friendship a deep desire for the Japanese was born in my heart, which I have never lost.

When the Lord granted me the privilege to raise up Bethany Chapel in Long Beach, California, my prayer and desire was that our church would raise up missionaries and send them to Japan. During those early days of prayer for Japan I heard of Missionary Leonard Coote and his many years of ministry so unselfishly given to the Japanese people. The trials he and his family suffered prior to the outbreak of World War II, and the testimonies of victory and deliverance, overwhelmed my heart. I felt I needed to meet and know this man personally.

As my search to know him and become acquainted with him continued, God laid his hand on one of our most promising young couples, calling them as missionaries to Japan. Having made our contact with Brother Coote, I asked if our young missionary candidates could come to the Ikoma Bible College in Japan. My prayer was for Brother Coote's pioneering spirit to seize them and that the passion and burden that so possessed him would fall on them.

This, in a great measure, happened. Truly, I had never met anyone who was as totally committed to the cause of missions as Leonard Coote.

My prayer is that everyone who reads this book will also be mightily moved upon by the Holy Spirit and receive something of the mantle of this man of God. Also, as you read this book, you will find one outstanding characteristic that can be summed up in just three words, "Never give up." That is why the title of this book is *Impossibilities Become Challenges*.

Leonard Coote, through faith, turned every stumbling stone into stepping stones, every test into a testimony. This book is a testament that Brother Coote stood in the vanguard of those who have been chosen by the Holy Spirit to finish writing the last chapter of "The Acts of the Apostles."

As you read about the journey of this giant of faith, I pray you will be overwhelmed with the same passion, dedication and desire of this "man of destiny"— that you, too, will commit yourself and whole heartedly dedicate your life towards reaching the lost with the glorious gospel of the Lord Jesus Christ.

David E. Schoch

REMARKS
(FROM THE FOURTH EDITION)

The bulk of the matter of the present book originally appeared in the first edition under the title "Twenty Years In Japan." This was revised and additional chapters added, with the new title "Twenty Five Years In Japan."

As many inquiries have come to hand for extra copies of the book, which has for a long time been out of print, I considered it wise to still further add extra chapters revealing that God's faithfulness, so markedly shown fifty years ago, has continued in times of war and in many other varying circumstances.

The new title is "Impossibilities Become Challenges" and the chapters have been increased to 37.

October 4th, 1965 will be the fifty second anniversary of my arrival in Japan and honor and praises are given unto His great and glorious Name.

May every reader be impressed with the fact which this book has endeavored to prove that His Word is true from the beginning.

Leonard W. Coote
Ikoma, Naraken, Japan

CONTENTS

1	Japan-Ward	1
2	Conviction and Conversion	7
3	Lining Up with the Word	12
4	Rebellion and Obedience	27
5	The Baptism of the Holy Ghost	34
6	First Evangelistic Experience	43
7	Call and Separation from Business	50
8	First Outpouring of the Spirit	57
9	The Outpouring Spreads to Other Cities	67
10	Marriage	76
11	Miraculous Supply of Needs	80
12	Studying the Language	92
13	The Yokohama Revival	96
14	The Great Japanese Earthquake	106
15	City of Osaka	125
16	Ikoma Bible School	127
17	First Time Leaving Japan	132
18	In the Lions' Den	140
19	Problems Met and Overcome	150
20	Bible School's First Graduation	160
21	Small Churches	163
22	On to Korea	166
23	Japan's Bible School, Second Wing	171
24	Visit to Australia & New Zealand	174
25	The Pacific War	176
26	Emmanuel Church & Revival Temple	184
27	International Bible College	186
28	Missions on the March	194
29	My Flying Visit to Japan	196
30	My Diary (First Week in Japan)	200
31	First New Missionaries	208
32	Post-War Activities	210
33	Osaka Evangelistic Tabernacle	213
34	Esther Coote's Coronation	218
35	South Korean Bible College	221
36	Taejon Evangelistic Tabernacle	223
37	Philippines Bible College	225
38	Breaking Forth	226

CHAPTER ONE

JAPAN - WARD

"How unsearchable are His judgments."
(Romans 11:33)

Well do I remember one Sunday evening after the ordinary chapel service at the local Methodist church in England, taking a stroll with two or three friends, saying to them, "Do you see yonder moon? It will not be many days before I shall be seeing that same moon from the opposite side of this earth," alluding to my going to Japan in a very short time.

After my finishing school, my father had gone to a good deal of expense to send me to a special private commercial school to finish my education. I was employed as a stenographer by a firm of shippers of cotton goods to China and Japan. One of the heads of this firm visited the orient every two or three years, and more as a joke, I had said many times that I would gladly accompany Mr. Hemingway and just be his boy, cleaning his shoes etc., if he would permit my going with him on his travels.

Little did I think at that time that God would in a remarkable manner open the way for me to visit the same land, and as a result would make my permanent home in the Far East.

I was at this time a very ambitious young man. Though working hard in the daytime, evenings would be employed in further study, endeavoring to excel in various lines of commercial life. At times I would spend every possible ounce of energy to prepare myself to compete for the championship of High Speed Shorthand writers in England, and at other times I was considering preparing to become a reporter in the House of Commons.

For this reason the public library was often visited and the news from various English towns scanned to see what openings presented themselves. Especially was the London Times daily newspaper looked into constantly to see if there was a need for a stenographer for Japan. For some reason I felt there was no possibility of receiving the position, but standing there as I was, I wrote a formal application.

Strange as it may have seemed, I received letters from the advertisers, which was the well known firm of Lever Brothers soap makers of Port Sunlight fame, and on no less than three occasions I visited Liverpool for interviews regarding the position.

As they paid my traveling expenses to and from Liverpool, the question of being employed and sent by them to Japan seemed to become very evident on the second visit, but this was followed by a letter stating that they had decided to send another young man just back from Africa, to Japan, so that the position was filled. Imagine my surprise some weeks later to receive another letter from the same firm asking for a further interview, and I well remember, though I was not at that time converted, kneeling down at my bedside asking for God's help and guidance when I had to make a decision to accept or reject their offer for the position in Japan.

I was the eldest of six children, and not one of us had ever left home. I had never been away from home, so the acceptance of the position brought a distinct break in the family circle of five boys and one girl, and father and mother had quite a hard time to reconcile themselves, but left the matter of going entirely with me to decide.

I was at that time a church going Christian, even a Sunday School teacher, and enthusiastic in all the departments of church work, but was without that change of heart - that renewal of mind - that "being born again" so definitely spoken of in God's Word as essential to enter the kingdom of heaven.

Not that there had been no strivings of the Spirit of God upon my heart, nor hungerings for reality in my own soul. As early as seven years of age I had experienced God's

JAPAN - WARD

Spirit drawing me close to Him.

One Sunday evening I and my younger brother were home. Father had gone to the evening service at the church. Without any apparent reason, I drew near to mother and explained to her that I felt strange. She sensed God moving upon me and said it must be God dealing with me, and she got me on my knees beside her to pray. The tears flowed, and can you imagine the picture, my brother and I both at my dear mother's knees praying? That was the first definite touch from God. Praise God for His faithfulness. His Spirit does strive with men! Beloved reader, have you experienced this touch from the other world? It is no sentimental passing fancy, but a divine reality: the Creator of all men wooing us unto Himself.

At this time of preparing for Japan I was still without a definite personal experience of salvation. God was again striving with me. Practically every Sunday morning as I entered the Methodist Church, I would bow in prayer and inwardly cry out to God for something to take place that day that would settle matters concerning my soul. Oh so many times I asked God to let the preacher say something that would give me inward peace and rest. But I never found that for which I craved.

And there was ever a longing in my heart for reality. As Saturday afternoons were free, I often stood in my bedroom upstairs gazing across the stretch of open fields, wondering why I had been born, what was the object of my life, and what would be the end of this existence? What wonderful material I was for a personal worker, but no one ever spoke to me about my soul.

Once when I was seventeen, in the evening service of the Methodist Church, I raised my hand as a decision for Christ. It was the third Sunday in October and the day set apart as a special effort to bring the young to Christ. I had a battle to raise my hand, but the moment I did, God flooded my soul with joy, but sad to say it this experience did not last long. There were so few among the members who had a real salvation experience, and when I saw church officers

4   IMPOSSIBILITIES BECOME CHALLENGES

smoking their pipes and cigars, and I observed the enthusiasm for socials and concerts to aid with church finances, but little excitement about praise and prayer meetings, what touch of God I did receive soon faded away.

I would, however, follow the sermons preached very religiously, and carefully, and by dint of willpower determined to put into practice what I heard that I might find peace, but without success. At this time I was becoming very discouraged. The powers of sin were making inroads into my life despite my good intentions and strong will. At one time I became so despondent over my spiritual condition and the lack of spiritual help, I even considered jumping into a lake and destroying my life. But this I was afraid to do, and God wonderfully prevented me from doing such a rash thing.

It is only right and fair to say, however, that seemingly efforts were made in the church I attended to give me that peace for which I so heartily longed. For a time, I studied theology with some other young men under the tutorship of the local preachers, but beloved reader, it was not theology that I needed, but a heaven born salvation - a work wrought in my being - a new spirit that can only be brought about by God Himself. Wesley Guilds and other associations were arranged and spiritual and scriptural subjects discussed, but just as water cannot lift above its level, so without the leaders of the church themselves having this second birth, I too, was not to receive soul satisfaction.

How strange it seems to say that during this time I was even teaching a Sunday School class, and would walk in the rain to prayer meeting to prove that I was earnestly seeking God.

Final preparations were made for the journey to Japan and goodbyes said to many relatives and friends. A farewell service was held at the Sunday School I attended and I was presented with a Bible as a parting gift. To avoid traveling on Sunday as much as possible, I left home a day earlier than was actually necessary, and waited at the southern port in England where I was to embark for the continent.

JAPAN - WARD

Well do I remember that last Sunday night on English soil. Before boarding the boat to take me to Holland in Europe I was attracted by the music of the Salvation Army band. Right there and then with the first touch of lonesomeness, I was ready for a good dose of salvation. I stood around the Army ring, and the music moved my soul. Tears filled my eyes, but no one spoke to me about my need, and again a personal worker's opportunity was lost.

A night's journey across the ocean brought me to Holland, and soon I was on the border of Germany, changing trains at Berlin for the Trans-Siberian Railway, bringing me to Russia, then to Siberia, and finally to Vladivostock. Another sea journey to Tsuruga, and lo and behold I was on the other side of the world, having traveled just ten days, and now was in the land of the rising sun.

Before leaving England many enquiries had been made regarding conditions in Japan, and much information had been gathered revealing that many young business men every year who go to the orient are soon overcome with temptation, filling a drunkard's grave. To avoid bad companionships and protect myself from such a disaster, I sought a room in the home of a missionary family. I had been given the name of a Missionary Home, run under the auspices of the Japan Evangelistic Band led by Rev. J.B. Thornton in Kobe. His home was to mean much to me spiritually in the days to come.

Reaching Kobe, Japan, at midnight, I put up at the Oriental Hotel, and presented myself to the Kobe office of Lever Brothers next morning, who had no word of my arrival and were indeed surprised to see me. I found out later that my going to Japan was a mistake, this happening in decoding a cable, so that for a long time I had nothing to do, and the possibility of being sent home again rather brought me into a despondent condition. But God makes no mistakes. "And the iron did swim" (2 Kings 6:6).

And now after fifty years I stop and praise the Lord as I realize that in the natural my arrival in Japan was through a mistake in decoding a cable, and that my arrival was a surprise to the managers of the Japan branch of Lever Brothers. How marvelous are God's ways! What a proof this incident is of the text "All things work together for good to them that love the Lord" (Romans 8:28). Oh if we would only realize that nothing happens by chance in this world. Even the mistakes of men are used by the Lord for the fulfilling of His divine will and purposes. Praise His name for evermore.

CHAPTER TWO

CONVICTION AND CONVERSION

*"He will reprove the world of sin, and
of righteousness, and of judgment."
(John 16:8)*

I had not been staying many days in the home of Rev.
Thornton, before I found out he was a man that believed
and lived the Word of God in its entirety. Daily in morning
family worship and in other prayer meetings he would invariably hold up the Bible and declare that he believed
every word, every chapter, yea, its whole contents, to be the
very breath of God in the original language. As he
emphasized this point day after day, I began to wonder if he
really meant it. I had been influenced to believe the Bible
might be a good book, but could not bring myself to accept
the fact that it was reliable in its entirety. Higher critics had
made me think the creation story of Genesis was merely a
fable, and the story of Jonah and the great fish another
fable, and so on.

I had not received such atheistic opinions from books
but from the pulpit of the church. What a crime it is that
the very church which should have been a soul saving institution had become an atheist creating body.

Brother Thornton, too, was definitely an American, and
I a very conservative Englishman. Some of his American
ways seemed strange, as I had never come in contact with
Americans before, and now that he insisted on declaring
that he believed the Bible to be the very Word of God
Himself, yea, the very breath of God in the original
language - well, to say the least, I really did think he was
very eccentric.

At the same time I was silently impressed with his godly
life. His congeniality, and the way he had taken me into his
home and acted as a father towards me, had won my heart.
I began to argue with him, and try to show him where I

8   **IMPOSSIBILITIES BECOME CHALLENGES**

thought he was wrong. Certain places in the Word were brought as proofs the Bible could not be fully relied on. His reply was ever the same: "Brother Coote, if you do not take the Bible as the revelation of God to man, that is allright, just leave it alone. We will not argue about it."

Brother Thornton knew the power and working of the Holy Spirit and that argument would only hinder. But I was not content. I still tried to argue, and ever received the same reply: "No Brother Coote, we will not argue. If you cannot see the Bible as God's revelation to man just leave it alone. It will make no difference to me. We will still remain friends."

I had now started on my five year contract with Lever Brothers. I was full of worldly ambitions, and being free from restraints, and facing new people, new scenes, coupled with the enjoyment of selfish pleasures and fleshly indulgences, were it not for the faithful, secret prayers of this dear brother, in a short time I would have filled a drunkard's grave.

Being a paying guest in the Missionary Home I came in touch with missionaries of all denominations from America, England, China and India. Frequently, meetings were held in English in the home by missionaries of the Japan Evangelistic Band. Particularly the ministries of Paget Wilkes and Barclay Buxton had a strange but holy effect on me. A converted man named C.B. Argall often stayed in the home and exerted a good influence on my life, but yet I was far from accepting the general doctrine that the Bible was actually God's Word.

The message on the cross of Christ had begun to make an impression on my soul. It wasn't that I had not heard it before, for I was familiar with the facts. But I began to wonder and to consider what a tremendous sacrifice Christ made, and that surely there was something greater in the truth of the cross than I had yet realized. The reason for the cross, and its results became a progressive subject of thought.

One night, feeling distressed about the question and

CONVICTION AND CONVERSION

wondering if the Bible were really and fully God's Word, and why Brother Thornton would not meet my arguments, I entered my bedroom so thinking, when suddenly I had an argument with myself. I said: "What right have you, Coote, to declare that the Bible is or is not the Word of God, when you have never read it through once? You are trying to argue with men who have read it through many times and have spent years teaching it. What if an English speaking Japanese were to belittle the writings of Shakespeare and it was found that such a critic had never read them through, what little weight would such criticism carry!" I saw myself foolish in my former actions, and then and there declared that I would read the whole Book through once, in order to place myself in the position of authority to argue about it.

I did not read the Book to find salvation, but to find the supposed inaccuracies I believed it contained. I began to read the Bible with a pencil in one hand and a note book in the other searching for mistakes. I began at Genesis, read through the five books of Moses; at times quite interested and at other times thinking it a dreary book; then I came to Joshua, Judges, the two books of Samuel, the Kings, followed by Chronicles, right on until I came to Jeremiah. Without any noticeable conviction I retired to my room after supper one night as usual, and continued reading the Bible at the place I had left off the previous evening. As I read the words

"The heart is deceitful above all things and desperately wicked; who can know it?" (Jeremiah 17:9),

I was smitten. I saw myself as I had never seen myself before: a lost, undone, wicked, hellbound sinner! It seemed as if my clothes smelt of the awfulness of sin; degradation was all around me, and the mouth of the pit was opened wide to receive me, body, soul and spirit.

I could do nothing but fall on my face and call on God to save my soul. But the more I prayed the worse I became and the more terrible did my sins appear. I prayed until I had to go to sleep without finding any joy or peace or satisfaction.

10   IMPOSSIBILITIES BECOME CHALLENGES

Though miserable all the next day, without telling anyone of the conviction on my soul, that next night I went quickly to my room and sought God with all my heart again. Feeling that God was getting further away from me, I prayed prostrating myself on the floor. But instead of finding relief it seemed that God had deserted me, and salvation could never be my portion.

A natural and proper thing would have been to go to my spiritual friend, Brother Thornton, and receive help and instruction on how to get rid of my burden, but the pride of my evil heart would not permit me to reveal my need to anyone. The deceitfulness of my heart had hidden my condition from myself, and now it would hide it from others, and so at every turn a man's heart becomes his chief enemy.

The third night I retired as quickly as possible to my room and sought God with all my heart. I remember taking up the carpets on the floor this night, feeling that I was not worthy to pray on carpets. I was as much away from God as ever, and the matter seemed hopeless. I was about to further humble myself by going outside to pray on the dirt in the backyard, when something arrested and stilled my mind. It was possibly a vision, for I seemed to be beholding the cross and the five bleeding wounds of Calvary. The blood pouring out from every part of His body was presented to me, and in a few minutes I seemed to understand this blood was for my sins.

Though there was no audible voice, I heard the words distinctly saying: "Coote, look and live!" I did so, and deep down into my heart was a stirring as if Jesus in very person was saying to me "I died thus for you - I shed my blood for your sins. Just accept my work of redemption." I did so crying out, "I believe! I believe!"

An inward peace now settled over my soul, and I continued to prostrate before God in silence, when suddenly the floodgates of my soul were opened; joy rushed in and I knew no bounds. Joy flooded my being as I realized that I had been converted, my sins were washed away, and now I

CONVICTION AND CONVERSION

was a child of God. Everything was different. The leaves on the trees the next morning had a different tint, and the office conditions seemed all changed.

To every member of the office, whether European or Japanese, I told the glad tidings that I had been converted and had found forgiveness of sins. They laughed at me, told me that I was already a missionary, and scoffed at me, but that made no difference. I had found God and laughing or scorning could not change what He had done.

With my spiritual eyes now open, I began to see the kind of men I was working with and the horrible dangers of strong drink, as well as the tremendous immorality existing everywhere in Japan. I had taken the precautions of having on my office desk a Bible and placing in my button hole a temperance badge. I had done this not because I accepted the Bible as the Word of God, but merely as a defense against invitations to go on drinking or immoral visits.

I had seen and heard plenty of proofs of the dangers to young men coming out from England to the Far East, proofs of the warning that I had received from folks in England who had been in Japan, and those received even from the Japanese consul himself residing in London. A very young Englishman who was working alongside me in this office told me how he was a Sunday School teacher when in England, but he boasted how he was dead drunk on his first evening in Japan. Another young man, a bookkeeper in the office, would groan again and again during office hours because of the pain in his body brought on by a disease he had obtained through immorality.

He Is The Light

CHAPTER THREE

LINING UP WITH THE WORD

*"He will reprove the world of sin, and
of righteousness, and of judgment."
(John 16:8)*

No sooner had real joy followed the assurance of sins forgiven than I heard a distinct voice say, "What about the Bible now?" Immediately I saw the point, and breaking before the Lord afresh I took my Bible, even kissing it, and declared it was the Word of God. All unbelief vanished, and the supposed inaccuracies that in my unconverted condition I was sure it contained entirely disappeared.

Praise the Lord I can truly say that every doubt and every argument about the so called inaccuracies in the Word utterly disappeared from my mind the moment that the flood of God's salvation entered my soul.

A second time I heard a voice asking me whether I would be willing to take the Word of God as my sole guide in life, and with my two hands laid on the open Bible, I vowed to God an irrevocable surrender to the Word wherever it led me, and whatever the results might be. I was so overtaken by the love of God and the power of the Spirit, I poured out my soul in words like "Sink or swim, live or die, failure or success, whether it means the creation of enemies or the loss of friends, I vow to read and reread the Word of God daily, and make my life an exact duplicate of the Bible in action."

How I have thanked God a thousand times over that He ever challenged me to take this stand. It has become a strong pull in my soul whenever there have been temptations to swerve from its teachings, and it has been a divine inspiration to press on into more and more of God's marvellous plans for His children.

The vow was meant in every detail and no sacrifice appeared too great to make to fulfill the same, but I was

LINING UP WITH THE WORD

13

entirely ignorant at that time of all the changes that would have to be made, and how far away from the Bible I was.

As I look back today and consider my condition at that time, though endeavoring to live an outwardly moral life, I was truly as far away from God and His plans and as ignorant of His principles as any heathen in a foreign land.

WATER BAPTISM

It was not long before my first test came. A baptismal service was to be held for some European converts and I was asked whether I would be baptized or not. Immediately I replied, "Oh, I have been baptized." Asked when, I told them just before leaving my homeland. My father believed in baptism by immersion and did not baptize his family as infants but left it to the individual conscience of each child as he grew up. Before departing for Japan my father asked me to be baptized, and to this I agreed. Since I did not know where I could be baptized by immersion, I had our Methodist Church pastor perform the ceremony of sprinkling my forehead after a morning worship service which, of course, was called baptism. So when I was asked to be baptized in Kobe I resented it as I felt I had been baptized. But I gave myself away when I replied, "Of course there are two ways of being baptized: one by immersion and the other by sprinkling, but I do not think it matters much as both ways are in the Bible."

My friend immediately said, "Show me where it is recorded in the Bible that they baptized folks by the so called sprinkling method, and the next time we meet you give me the chapter and verse." I was sure that I could do this in a short time, but received my first shock when after hunting all the way through the Bible with a concordance, I could not find one instance where people were sprinkled. On the contrary, I read passage after passage showing how men went down into the water and came up out of the water, as shown in Matthew 3:16 and John 3:23, which says:

14   IMPOSSIBILITIES BECOME CHALLENGES

"John also was baptizing in Aenon, near to Salem, because
there was much water there."

Though I was convicted by this study that the scriptural
method of baptism was immersion as opposed to sprinkling,
I was not able to humble myself and obey the Word. It was
as if the Lord beckoned with His hand and said, "Coote
come along take your first step," but I was being pulled
back by various sentiments. The devil whispered in my ear,
"Did you not go forward on that Sunday morning in the
Methodist Church in the old country with a true heart, and
a seriousness to be baptized? What will that pastor think
and the congregation before whom you were baptized,
when they hear you have gone back on your baptism?"

For quite a long time I see-sawed to and fro. First the
Lord would beckon and say, "Come along obey your vow.
Did you not say sink or swim, loss or gain, that you would
obey the Word at any cost?" Then the devil would appeal
to my sense of honor that I actually went through the
ceremony in England honestly, and how could I go back on
it now?

Finally one evening, Sister Taylor of Kobe showed me
the Word where it says,

"If we walk in the light ... we have fellowship one with
another, and the blood of Jesus Christ His Son
cleanseth us from all sin" (1 John 1:7).

The Spirit of God revealed to me that to be baptized by
immersion was new light and by obeying the Word I was
actually walking in the light.

The next day I was willing to obey God's Word, keep my
vow and was immersed in water in the Japanese Baptist
Church in Kobe.

What a day this was! How well I remember it! I was
baptized with two other men, one an American, and the
other a Scotchman. Brother Thornton had been having
meetings for Europeans on Sunday afternoons in the Kobe
Baptist Church and a real spirit of enquiry had been
manifested among the Europeans. The American who was
one of those baptized was certainly a hard case. He had

LINING UP WITH THE WORD
15

been in Japan for a period of over 20 years, and to such depths of depravity had he gone that he earned his living by trapeze work for a Japanese circus. However, his immoral ways had ruined his body and he could no longer follow even this calling. His whole body was simply filled with disease. He sought the Lord and God heard him. Many falls he had, however, and later on we heard how the Lord took him home to Himself, in the faith. Such a taste had he for strong drink that he would often be so drunk in the morning that he would only be able to get down stairs by letting his body fall down the stairs, as he was unable to walk down.

His desire for liquor knew no bounds. If he had no money, naturally the poison would not be sold to him, and on one occasion being unable to buy what he wanted and thinking a bottle of red ink on the counter was whiskey he grabbed the bottle and drank all.

My other companion in water baptism was a younger man, a fine looking young Scotchman, but he too had known the very depths of sin and depravity. He told me that he had committed every possible and known sin, even suicide itself. Strange it may seem that he still lived for he had actually tried to commit suicide, cutting his throat by a broken beer bottle and was only brought back to life again through the persistence of a doctor.

And these were my fellows in water baptism. On my right one whose body reeked with disease, and on my left one who had even committed murder and suicide. And yet, I, who had never known the taste of drink or these out-broken sins was possibly the worst of them all, for I believe the Word teaches us that the sins of the heart, unbelief, pride and a Pharisaical life, to be worse abomination in God's sight than the sins of the flesh.

The joy that I received on being baptized was as great, if not greater, than when I had been converted. Brother Thornton in his weekly messages had been speaking of receiving the baptism of the Spirit, and linking this experience with that of water baptism. I remember how on

IMPOSSIBILITIES BECOME CHALLENGES

leaving the water I exercised my will and received the blessing by faith, and because a certain feeling came into my soul I was sure that I had received the baptism. But I soon found out that this was not the fullness as revealed in the Acts of the Apostles.

TITHING

I really thought that now I had graduated. The victory had been won although I had stubbornness for a long time, but little did I realize that this was but the beginning of several similar battles. For no sooner had the victory about immersion been won than the hand of the Lord again was seen beckoning to me to take another step forward.

About this time I was impressed again and again by reading about "tithes" in the Word of God. I showed my utter ignorance of spiritual things when I say that I had to find out the meaning of tithes before I came into the realization that God's way of supporting His work was for the believer to use one tenth of his income for spiritual work.

My second battle began right there. God's hand again beckoned me to step forward and obey the Word. This seemed a tremendous mountain. "Fancy," I thought, "to give one tenth of all I receive, one tenth of my income to God's work - why that is preposterous!" And yet there was no doubt now in my mind that the Word clearly taught it. Again I was between two seas. On the one hand my vow to obey the Word, and on the other my great ambition to get together all the money that I could possibly save for the future.

I argued that my income was really too large to tithe. Were I still in England where my income was only a third or fourth of what it was now, it would be an easy matter to obey the Lord, but my salary now was considerably more than I had ever received before in my life, and to give exactly one tenth of this to God, it was so large that it seemed to be an impossibility. (How easily the devil tries to deceive

LINING UP WITH THE WORD

God's people! Since coming into God's service how many believers argue just the other way about, feeling that because their income is so small that they cannot possibly tithe; I, feeling that my income was too large, and others that their income is too small.)

Then I said to myself, I do not like this mechanical, set way of giving to God. I want to give when I feel like it. It may be when I am really wonderfully blessed I will give more than one tenth. Here again how clever the devil is, because he knows that if he can get God's people to act on scriptural lines only when they feel like it, he has a way to weaken God's cause, for he is able to bring all kinds of feelings and conditions about whereby believers will be against obeying the Lord.

What would happen to this world if the farmer only sowed his grain when he felt like it, or the postman only delivered our letters when he felt in good spirits?

Praise the Lord He has shown me that the tithing of our income is not giving something to God, but it is returning to God that which already belongs to Him. We do not give the rents of our houses to the landlord; it is his by right of being the owner. And so is tithing with God, and the offerings are the freewill gifts that we make to God's cause because of His great love to us in redemption.

As I began to lose my joy and fellowship with God I knew that I would have to do something.

To obey outright seemed to be impossible, and so I made a compromise. I was sending home for the support of my parents a certain amount every month, and I decided that I would reckon half of that amount as tithe. But I only did this for one month. At the close of the month I felt so mean and wretched that I simply broke through and said, "I will obey the Word, keep my vow and be true to God." Praise the Lord, then the joy of the Lord filled my soul.

SPIRITUAL DIFFICULTIES

It is so easy in writing a record of God's dealing with one's own soul to show only the happy side of things. This has a tendency to discourage others who, reading the record, endeavor to seek blessing and inspiration for their own lives. I must therefore be true and not only state the ways in which God definitely revealed Himself to me, but also show how I was often in despondency through my own faults and weaknesses; in discouragement because I could not understand the Word though I was systematically reading it day by day; in doubt because my faith in Christ was bringing me more and more opposition from fellow workers in the office and I was realizing that I was being isolated because of my stand for Christ.

DESPONDENCY OVER FAULTS
AND WEEKNESSES

It was only natural that all my faults and weaknesses should be revealed to me in a definite way. Every morning as I awakened from sleep I would praise God and then open His Word, praying that he would open my eyes and make me to see the reality of His truth. After reading I would meditate on the Word and see wherein my life was not in accordance with it. It was to be expected therefore that my faults and weaknesses would appear to be multiplied, and the enemy of my soul, ever ready to stop my spiritual progress, would endeavor to plant doubts in my mind by saying, "If you were fully converted why should you have that fault, and see how weak you are on that line? There must be something wrong with your salvation."

And are not many young converts disturbed on this point? When a baby is born it is far from perfect. Think of all the schooling, training, learning and experiences that it must go through before it becomes a fully grown adult. So it is with the new convert recently born of God. Moreover, the spiritual growth is even more complicated for we have

LINING UP WITH THE WORD

19

to undo, dig out, even root out traits of the old man, tendencies to the flesh and to the world, besides growing in grace and in the knowledge of God.

DISCOURAGEMENT BECAUSE I COULD NOT FULLY UNDERSTAND THE WORD

I had been influenced to a definite system in reading the Word. By reading five chapters daily from the Old Testament and three chapters from the New Testament I could read through the Old testament once and the New Testament twice in a year. But I was a babe in Christ. Some of the Old Testament records, chronologies and histories were so dry. I had not yet been awakened to see the underlying principles. I had not yet acquired a taste for finding Christ among the types and shadows of the Old Testament. I was tempted to feel it was no use to continue reading. Brother Thornton ever spurred me on. "Read even though you do not know what you are reading. Do not attempt to study what you read, just read, and you will find that the bare reading of the Word will be a great blessing to you," he ever urged.

DOUBT FROM OPPOSITION TO THE FAITH

Doubts prevailed because my faith in Christ was bringing more and more opposition. I soon found out that there was only one course to take regarding spiritual matters in the office where I was employed. I was either to be an out and out Christian or a mere nominal one inwardly, and just be one of the crowd. Moreover, I soon saw that I could not retain even a nominal allegiance to Christ if I made the other fellow workers in the office my friends and did as they did. God enabled me to choose the out and out course. I was laughed at, ostracized and became the center of all fun and jokes. Such a condition was hard to bear and I felt the loneliness of it, especially on holidays and on Saturday

IMPOSSIBILITIES BECOME CHALLENGES

afternoons when, without a friend or acquaintance with whom I could have any fellowship or recreation, I found myself entirely alone. I remember my father at this time writing to me saying that now he realized I had actually become a real Christian, for the persecution of which I wrote proved it to him.

As I look over these days now, I must thank God afresh for the isolation, loneliness and dark tunnel experiences. They drove me to God and prepared the way for the Spirit of God to enter into my heart. Not being preoccupied with even legitimate recreation and pastimes I was a candidate to see the needs of thousands around me. God was able to use me, even without the language and before I became a missionary in the distribution of not merely a few thousand tracts, but hundreds of thousands of them.

THE SECOND COMING

But the end was not yet. Questions regarding the second appearing of Christ were brought strongly to my conscience. The doctrine seemed so opposed to reason and to ordinary ways of living that I could not possibly feel it was a genuine truth. About this time, however, someone handed me a book by W. E. Blackstone, entitled "Jesus is Coming." As I looked up the Bible references and saw how clearly my ideas about the world getting better were entirely opposite to the teaching of the Word, I was again shocked and the Spirit showed me clearly how foolish it was to live just to make money, or for a name, when at any moment the trumpet might sound and Jesus appear in the skies.

The joy of waiting for Jesus was now my portion. One day the Spirit stopped me in front of the large bookcase in my room. Inwardly, I seemed to hear a voice saying, "Suppose the Lord came tonight, how many books would you leave as a testimony for the Lord Jesus Christ?" I was shocked as my eye went from book to book, and I realized how little of the contents of my little library would ever lead

LINING UP WITH THE WORD

hungry souls to Christ.

Then and there without a moment's hesitation I decided to get rid of every book which did not have a distinct testimony to Christ. These were bound books. The devil whispered, "Better sell them to a second hand dealer for a little money." Immediately I rebuked him and took the books to a baker and had him throw them into the furnace for me. And so another victory was won.

DIVINE HEALING

Perhaps no other point was harder for me to obey the Lord in than that of trusting God for my body. In the daily reading of the Word I was becoming more and more convinced that God desired His people not to trust in the medicines, but in faith and prayer. Verses such as these seemed so clear:

"I will put none of these diseases upon thee, which I have brought upon the Egyptians, for I am the Lord that healeth thee" (Exodus 15:26).

"Is any sick among you? Let him call for the elders of the church; and let them pray over him, anointing him with oil in the name of the Lord: And the prayer of faith shall save the sick, and the Lord shall raise him up" (James 5:14,15).

I was absolutely convinced as to what the Word taught on this matter, but I had a natural aversion to what was known as Faith Healing, or Diving Healing. It seemed to me at that time that it was all mythical, a sort of trusting in nothing, and so I did not accept the truth. But God's Spirit is ever faithful, and again and again I would come across portions of the Word confirming this truth. The Lord this time seemed to be silently beckoning me to trust Him.

It must be remembered, of course, that I was absolutely ignorant of divine healing. What I did know, or what the terms bore to my mind, I only gathered from conversations between missionaries who had stayed, or were staying, in

IMPOSSIBILITIES BECOME CHALLENGES

the Missionary Home. I really had no knowledge that among Full Gospel people there was a general belief in God to heal.

The vow I had made at my conversion was brought to my memory again, and great conviction seized me that I was once more allowing my stubborn nature to come between my soul and God. And yet I felt I could not take the stand. Then I seemed to find a way out of the difficulty, and reasoned that I was seldom seriously sick, had a comparatively strong constitution, and therefore it was not necessary to come out plainly and take my stand for divine healing.

But it was not long before I was brought into a tight corner. Praise the Lord for the corners He brings His people into to teach them absolute obedience to His Word. It was in the summer time, and Japan's summers are really hot and hard to bear! The missionary that I was staying with had gone away for the summer, leaving me with a yardman who helped me get my meals.

One day I was completely overcome with an attack of something inwardly that I had never experienced before. The intensity of the attack really made me afraid. My whole system was bilious. I had dysentery and was altogether faint. Right away my thought was, "Oh, I wish I had taken the stand on divine healing when I was well. It would have been easier to believe the Lord now."

I decided to go and see a European doctor. He bade me strip off all my clothing, and he gave me a thorough examination, asking me to watch a pain that I had in my right side, and to return to him that same evening.

The pain increased in intensity and I was in such agony during that afternoon in my office that I could not wait until evening, but managed to get to his office by a Japanese rickshaw. A second time the doctor examined me, and almost immediately declared, "You have an acute attack of appendicitis. You must be operated on immediately." I was dumbfounded. The thought of an immediate operation, of my body being placed under the knife of a doctor just at a time when I had wavered to step out on the

LINING UP WITH THE WORD

promises of God, and knowing that I was not playing true to the vow I had made to change my life to whatsoever I found in the Word, really made me afraid.

Not only was I dumbfounded but in the two or three moments that followed I saw as clearly as if I were seeing lantern slides, a nurse leaning over my still body on the operating table and shaking her head, indicating that there was no hope. Immediately the scene changed and a telegraph messenger boy opened the garden gate of my home in England, and my mother hurriedly opened the telegram which read, "Leonard passed away yesterday, appendicitis operation unsuccessful." Throwing her apron over her head she burst out in tears and at this point I stamped my foot in the doctor's office and said, "It cannot be done." The doctor was more than a little disturbed. "Look here, young man," he said, "did you not come to me with your body in pain, and have not I diagnosed the trouble? I tell you if you do not have this operation right away you will be a dead man in a week. I cannot even guarantee that you will live that long."

I realized that I had acted rudely, and poorly. I partly excused myself that it was impossible to take the next train as suggested as I would have to go to the bank next morning for the train fare. The doctor finally agreed to allow me to go right home that night and he would call at my office, arranging for the finances for the journey to Tokyo, 300 miles away, and that he would wire St. Luke's Hospital for an automobile to meet my train so that I could be operated on right away after my arrival.

I agreed to go right home and to bed, feeling I had a few minutes, at any rate, to settle the question of divine healing with my Lord. On the way home I wired my missionary friend to come immediately. He arrived in the early hours of the morning. I requested him to obey Mark 16:17 and 18,

"And these signs shall follow them that believe ... they shall lay hands on the sick and they shall recover."

This he did and immediately faith gripped my heart with the

24 IMPOSSIBILITIES BECOME CHALLENGES

assurance that God had honored his and my faith.

It was not very long before the "toot toot" of the doctor's automobile horn was heard on the outside. He had come as promised to take me to the train for Tokyo for the operation. Soon I heard his heavy footsteps on the staircase, and with a hearty "Well how are you?" he entered the room.

"I am healed." I declared. The doctor just laughed at me. "Healed?" he asked, and then laughed again. Laugh or no laugh, I knew I was healed. "You are afraid of an operation, and afraid to die," he accused. I replied, "Doctor, I am not afraid to die for I know the blood of Jesus has cleansed me from all sin, but I have been failing God in not trusting Him for the healing of my body. My friend here has just prayed according to Mark 16:18, and I believe as a result I am healed."

Throwing back the bedclothes, I continued, "Doctor, here is the same body I brought to you yesterday. Examine me again. If I am healed, and you tell me so, all right, but if I am not healed you will know it." The doctor saw I was in my right mind and quite definite in my stand and fully honest about the matter.

Taking off his coat and rolling up his shirt sleeves, he began to examine my body again, paying particular attention to the side where the pain had been. He literally hit me more than once to see if he could not create a pain, continuing to ask me, "Are you sure you have no pain?"

Finally, he put on his coat again, and feeling for his hat, he said, "I will go to the post office right away and cancel the bed I wired for you at the hospital. You do not need an operation. The hospital officials would call me a fool if I sent you there. Good-bye."

And though nearly forty-five years have past since this incident, the trouble has never returned, and the Lord has ever proven Himself to be my healer.

And I would not be praising the Lord sufficiently if I did not also say that during the fifty years of continual residence in Japan I have enjoyed better health than the

LINING UP WITH THE WORD

average man or woman. Japan has a treacherous climate, and scores of missionaries and businessmen are compelled year after year to give up their vocation in this land for health reasons. I have lived a very strenuous life, and while there have been a few times when I have been confined to my bed, in every time of need as I have humbled myself at the foot of the cross, the blood of Jesus Christ has not only cleansed my soul, but healed my body, and today after fifty years in this land I believe I am as healthy as I ever was. But let not the reader be influenced to be fanatical along these lines. Read much of the word of God, and imbibe the spirit of the same, for I am sure you will be led to know that divine health is better than divine healing. The standard that I take is to walk as far as I possibly can in the will of the Lord. If I do this I expect God to grant to me strength, physical and mental, for the duties of the day. Should I find that I am ailing and something is wrong with my body, then I realize that in some way I have not used wisdom, and quietly waiting on the Lord, I search my heart, plead the precious blood, and believe God to bring me back to a normal condition.

On one occasion do I specially remember that God did not give the faith to meet the illness immediately. It was during the world-wide epidemic of influenza. I was laid down very heavily with it. For days I was absolutely gripped with a raging fever, but my soul dwelt in God. God had a higher purpose for me at that time. As I lay on my bed day after day God spoke to me clearly in visions, and the lessons I then learned I could not have received had I not been confined to the bed.

The time came, however, for faith to be exercised. Although confined to the bed for several days I had not been attended by a doctor neither had I taken any medicine. But I felt that I should go to a certain meeting in the evening. There was not the slightest doubt about this leading being the Lord, and I was assured that I was not attempting anything in my own strength. I arose from the bed and my whole body trembled as my fever was high and my body was terribly weak. To have done this in my own strength or by my own will power would have probably resulted in my death. But God gave me the faith, and bade me do it, and therefore the results were of a miraculous nature.

The journey to be taken from my home to the little mission was quite a distance, and what would take me about half an hour now took two hours. I was unable to stand upright without any help, but merely pushed my body forward while leaning against the sides of a house. I eventually arrived at my destination just as weak and the fever as high as before. However, the moment I reached the platform every bit of weakness and fever entirely left me, and I never felt healthier or better in my life. Though momentary in its coming this blessing was not just for the moment. It continued right on after the meeting and throughout the coming days.

CHAPTER FOUR

REBELLION AND OBEDIENCE

"Behold, to obey is better than sacrifice,
and to hearken than the fat of rams."
(1 Samuel 15:22)

How quickly men become puffed up! No sooner had the dealings of God along the lines of Divine Healing, the Second Coming and Tithing become realities in my spiritual walk, than I truly thought I had gone all the way with God, and there were no more things with which God must deal with me. In this attitude I was again to be shocked as God brought me slightly at first, and then more definitely, the verse recorded in Matthew 6:19:

"Lay not up for yourselves treasures upon earth,
where moth and rust doth corrupt, and where
thieves break through and steal, but lay up
for yourselves treasures in heaven" (Matthew 6:19).

Surely but slowly, the Spirit of God made me to know this was a new step of obedience required because of my vow to be according to God's Word in every detail. As conviction grew, my natural self began to rebel. I sought all manner of ways to compromise, trying to avoid having to obey again.

I even looked for the real meaning of the phrase "lay up" in the dictionary. I hoped that maybe it was an old English phrase with a different meaning than that placed on it today. The dictionary gave me no satisfaction, saying it was like putting something on a chair, or laying it away somewhere.

I was entirely opposed to the principle involved. As a young man on the threshold of life, with the responsibility of the eldest son, and feeling my duty toward the support of my parents, I felt it was not only impossible, but absolutely absurd. I argued that I should be making preparations for marriage, and should be saving funds toward that.

28   IMPOSSIBILITIES BECOME CHALLENGES

At that time I was the only certified teacher of Pitman's Shorthand in Japan, and if I ever intended to go into business for myself, some capital would be demanded. I was 11,000 miles from home at the opposite side of the globe, a stranger in a strange land. Added to this, my childhood training was to always save a penny out of every shilling, or five cents out of every dollar. The economical strain in my makeup rebelled when the finger of God pointed to Matthew 6:19 and beckoned me to make one more step along the pathway of life and lay not up treasures on earth.

This verse brought a real crisis into my life. God reminded me that I had entered into an irrevocable vow to take the naked Word of God and make it my own, and now it was my duty to walk in the further light of Matthew 6:19. I became so convicted, and yet so rebellious about it, I lost my joy and peace, though not my actual faith in God. For some time I had to skip Matthew the 6th chapter when reading the Bible. I read the Word consecutively, and as I finished the New Testament and would start in again at Matthew, the devil would whisper, "Now be careful, you are near that sixth chapter," and I would jump to the seventh chapter for I felt I could not obey Matthew 6:19, hoping to save myself from further conviction.

But God has gracious ways of dealing with the human soul. It was about then that I first came into contact with promise boxes. It was at the home of Sister Shepherd whom I was visiting, and one of those boxes was handed to me after a meal in order to take a promise. I opened the box and my little card read:

"Lay not up for yourselves treasures upon earth, where moth and rust doth corrupt, and where thieves break through and steal" (Matthew 6:19).

"Oh!" I thought. "That verse again!" But I still had no intention to obey, and felt it was utterly impossible to do so. But on another occasion, while visiting another English home, I was admiring the beautifully hand painted large framed mottoes on the wall, when suddenly my eyes caught one which seemed more beautiful than the rest, and these

REBELLION AND OBEDIENCE 29

words shined out at me:

"Lay not up for yourselves treasures upon earth,
where moth and rust doth corrupt, and where thieves
break through and steal" (Matthew 6:19).

Though I knew the Lord was bringing this verse forcefully to my conscience, I was still not ready to be true to the vow I had made when I was converted, and my stubborn will continued to rule.

Hitherto God had been leading. His Spirit had been lovingly inviting me to take my stand on His Word. But now I had rejected, and God saw that judgment would have to be used to bring me back to my senses, enabling me to humble myself again as I did when I first entered into that covenant.

Brother Thornton and I had arranged to go to Korea together to a convention where he was the special speaker. This was during my holidays, and I was going along to help by prayer. Just before embarking, he asked if I could make a loan sufficient to cover his fare as he would receive this at the close of the convention. I agreed, and together we went to the railway station. But when I felt for my wallet, it had entirely disappeared. A rigid search and informing the police was all of no avail. No one had been near me, and the possibility of losing it or having it stolen seemed out of the question.

A strange feeling came over my soul. I realized how careful I had been, how painstaking to watch every penny, and it was a shock to have such a large sum disappear in a few seconds. Then the point of the controversy of Matthew 6:19 loomed vividly in my mind, and in letters of red I saw:

"Lay not up for yourselves treasures upon earth
where moth and rust doth corrupt and where
thieves break through and steal."

Yet I was unable to step out in true faith and obedience. The convention was over and I was back at work. The summer heat was intense and I sought relief on week ends by visiting my friends at Arima, a small village among the hills near Kobe. By going right after Saturday morning's

30 IMPOSSIBILITIES BECOME CHALLENGES

work, I could leave again Monday morning, going straight to the office and have at least one day and a half of respite from the intense heat.

One day I arranged for the yard man to bring to the railway station a suitcase with my toilet articles, change of clothes, etc. Arriving at the station with only a couple of minutes to spare I was glad to see my man was there on time with my suitcase. When he saw me, he bent down to pick it up when his face changed color and he became terribly embarrassed. "What's wrong?" I asked. "I came here about fifteen minutes ago and set down your suitcase right here by my side, but now it's gone", he said. Again, a strange sensation came over my soul, but saying nothing, I jumped into the train without the suitcase and my missionary friend was waiting for me at the other end.

His first words were, "Brother Coote, where is your suitcase?" I replied miserably, "I do not know." Surprised, he must have thought me a little strange, for how could I possibly stay the week end without fresh clothes?

Finally, on hearing my story, he pointed right at me and said "Coote, to your knees. This is God!" Referring to the former loss of money, and as if an angel confirmed what he said, the words of Genesis 41:32 came to my mind:

"And for that the dream was doubled unto Pharaoh twice; it is because the thing is established by God, and God will shortly bring it to pass."

A fear of oncoming judgment now gripped my being. Battling through on my knees, I finally said yes to God one night, with my bank account laid on the bed, and the Bible opened at Matthew 6:19. I cried to God for His mercy and forgiveness for such a stubborn will, and begged His wisdom for the life's savings that had so far accumulated in the bank.

My new stand was that until the end of my business contract, as I received my salary, I would offer it to Him for His blessing and direction. Then I would first take out the one tenth as His tithe, using this for the support of the local work. Next, I arranged a liberal amount to cover my own

REBELLION AND OBEDIENCE

living expenses and the amount to be sent home to my parents, and the balance I would offer to God for His guidance as to how to dispose of the same.

I shall always remember how light I felt the morning after the crisis had passed, and I was once again filled with the joy of the Lord. But the devil is never silent. He now teased me that I would not have time to get the money out of the bank and use it for God. He made me fear the bank would crash right away. How cunning is the devil, and how he can change his tune to suit circumstances!

I did not distribute all of my savings immediately. It was simply handed over to God and daily His will was sought for its disposal. But the wonderful part is, there was no quibbling about giving it to Him. Before I had yielded the point, I would often have arguments with my conscience by saying, I am not laying up treasure for myself - maybe some day I will go to Bible School after my business contract is ended. But finally I realized that even these arguments were merely an evasion of the real issue.

Some of the most remarkable answers to prayer came in regard to the disposal of these funds. On one occasion I received a letter from India stating how the missionary there was believing God for a certain amount. Just when his faith was tested to the utmost, and discouragement defied him, my letter and check arrived!

What a joy it was, week after week to receive letters from the Belgian Congo, South Africa, India, China, and various parts of Japan acknowledging offerings, and to read how the offering met specific needs! Praise the Lord from Whom all blessings flow!

One incidence stands out more distinctly than any other. It happened when I was especially busy at the office. Special managers had arrived from England for reorganization and I had an important deadline to meet with reports, etc. Just the month before, I had emptied my savings all but thirty yen. Around the tenth of the month on a Friday, I felt the Lord directing me to send this thirty yen to Brother Taylor of Kobe. I was perfectly willing, but having already sent them some earlier that month, I hesitated. Still, the leading to send the money was strong. An inner conflict arose which began to hinder my work in the office, as my attention kept being distracted. Going downstairs, I shut myself up in a room and definitely cast the burden on the Lord, asking Him to keep me from making a mistake. Almost instantly the thought came to me, "If the same conviction returns to you at four o'clock today, then it is of God; if not, it is not from the Lord." With this the burden left and I was able to continue my work.

At noon I went home for lunch and returned to the office with the morning's experience forgotten, until the office clock struck four, and then from a distance a voice said inside me: "Send Taylor." That was enough. Out came the check and enclosing a very short note, I mailed it that day.

That was Friday afternoon. I received a short note of acknowledgment Sunday afternoon in which Brother Taylor stated he had arranged a baptismal service for some new converts from the slum district for Saturday morning. The devil had tried to tease him all day Friday about his having nothing at all to either pay his own fare or the carfare of the converts, and how foolish he would appear when he would have to tell them almighty God Whom he had preached to them had failed to supply his needs for the service. However, he went to rest Friday evening with the assurance God would honor his faith, and at breakfast Saturday morning, my letter containing the thirty yen arrived with sufficient time to go to the bank, cash it, and be back in time to take the converts to the baptismal service. How wonderful is our great God!

I cannot help but think how wonderful it is to be able to trust God implicitly. I had not the slightest way of finding out that this money was needed at this time, but as faith was exercised by the one needing it, and as I was living a fully surrendered life, God was able to make the need known, and lead to the sending of the check just in time. When we consider the varying needs in God's work at home and abroad, how wonderful it is to be able to live a life so

REBELLION AND OBEDIENCE

yielded to Him that He is able to speak and say "Send a few shillings here, or a few dollars there," just at the right time for the offering to arrive when it is needed.

Are there not many Christians in the homeland who bemoan their age or other ties which prevent them from offering themselves to the foreign field who could so yield themselves to the Lord and become a steward of material things? This in turn would bring them the same extreme joy of knowing that their hard earned pounds and dollars had been directed by the Lord as to meet financial crisis in India, Africa or the islands of the sea, or wherever God directed.

CHAPTER FIVE

THE BAPTISM OF THE HOLY GHOST

*"And it shall come to pass afterward, that I will
pour out of my Spirit upon all flesh."
(Joel 2:23)*

During the various meetings held for English speaking people in Kobe, I had come in contact with the teaching of the baptism of the Holy Ghost. I had also visited a number of conventions held at various times for the Japanese and had been convicted of my need to receive the baptism of the Spirit.

I had obeyed the teaching that I received on the subject, such as confession of all known sins, giving to God a complete surrender, and then by faith believing God grants the gift. I had also two or three times testified that I had received the blessing, but had never known the experience referred to in the second chapter of Acts, and the fourth verse: "And they were all filled with the Holy Ghost, and began to speak with other tongues as the Spirit gave them utterance."

Among the conversation of some, much was being made about speaking with tongues. I had even met one or two who were known to speak with other tongues, but I was not affected by this at all. I thought how foolish it was to discuss questions about speaking with tongues, for what use, I thought, was tongues anyhow?

However, my missionary friend was particularly burdened about a convention being held for the Japanese in the northern part of Japan. He did not have the fare to go. After prayer I knew the Lord wanted me to make it possible for him to visit the convention. This he did, and there he met God in a wonderful way. He came back all on fire, especially concerning the baptism of the Holy Ghost, and immediately started meetings in his own home for English speaking people. His one message was Acts 1. He did not

THE BAPTISM OF THE HOLY GHOST

emphasize speaking in tongues, but the urgent need of all Christians to know that they had been baptized with the Spirit.

He himself had not received the Pentecostal baptism, but a mighty anointing of God. When I saw him on his return from the convention, I was afraid of him. Something in his countenance looked me through and through. Nightly God worked in wonderful ways. Worship and much praise pervaded the meetings. Some who had not come in at the beginning were distinctly convicted at the first meeting they attended.

My own need was apparent. I saw clearly that I had to have an experience whereby I knew that I had been baptized in the Spirit, according to the scriptures. I had sought, and had taken it by faith many times. Then I wondered whether I had received it or not. I saw how clearly the disciples knew when they received the baptism. There was no possibility of doubt afterward. I could never look back and say on that day, or at that place I received the baptism.

My hunger increased. Everything else was dropped. One thing alone possessed my whole nature, and that was to have a scriptural experience, being baptized with the Holy Ghost, and to say with the apostles that the Holy Ghost had fallen on me.

The nightly meetings continued for some time. Many were blessed, inspired and encouraged, but I do not remember anyone testifying that they had received the definite experience of the baptism. Then the meetings closed, and oh how hungry I was! How disappointed I was! Where could I seek for reality? My whole being panted for God. At this time, Sisters Shepherd and Taylor who had received the baptism of the Spirit, invited me to visit their homes, and along with two other brethren, one a Jew, (Brother Newmark), and one a Greek, we sought the baptism of the Spirit once a week.

It is interesting how these meetings became longer and longer. At first we finished around 9 p.m., then it went until

IMPOSSIBILITIES BECOME CHALLENGES

10 p.m., then I remember having to run to catch the last tram home. Then we experienced having to walk home. Later we arrived home at three in the morning. Then, just in time for breakfast, and later, we went straight from the prayer meeting to the office. My soul was distinctly deepened by these meetings which ran over a period of six months or more but, as I never experienced the incoming of the Holy Ghost, I was often discouraged.

I spent my whole holiday of a week with a Free Methodist missionary in Arima to give myself to pray for the baptism. Before breakfast, after breakfast, and after lunch I would go to the hills and pray until the next meal. At first my friend felt a little concerned and asked me why I was praying so much. When I told him, he tried to show me that I had already received the baptism of the Spirit, but I knew I had not, for I had been placing my finger on Acts two, and I knew that the disciples knew when they received, and I felt I would know too when I received.

The second time he approached me, concerned about my desperate praying, he said off handedly, "Oh, you are seeking tongues!" I did not associate this with general conversations I had heard about tongues and asked him what he meant. He then told me of certain groups of people in America who lose their minds and fill the insane asylums. "Well," I said, "You have no need to fear along that line about me. I am not seeking tongues. I am seeking the outpouring and the infilling with the Holy Ghost."

Not long after this I began rereading the book of Acts and was particularly impressed with Acts 2:4:

"And they were all filled with the Holy Ghost
and began to speak with other tongues
as the Spirit gave them utterance."

I did not then receive the full satisfaction that I should speak with tongues, but the more I studied the Word the more I saw that those in Bible times did, and I was out for a Bible experience. I remember how my stand became "tongues, or no tongues, I must be baptized with the Spirit as on the day of Pentecost."

THE BAPTISM OF THE HOLY GHOST   37

Prior to my coming to Japan I had never known there was such an experience to be received by ordinary Christians. Possibly I might have known that saints of the Old Testament were empowered by the Spirit of God, but I do not ever remember any sermon, or address, or any article which gave any hint that God was pouring out His Spirit upon common believers today as He did on the day of Pentecost. The baptism of the Spirit was referred to in the above mentioned conventions held by the holiness people, more or less as a result of being sanctified, but as holiness was emphasized, my mind was still very vague about an individual experience of the baptism with the Spirit.

There were three of us seeking for the Spirit, literally day and night. For three months each of us went through Saturday nights praying, fasting and believing God to honor His Word. The three of us were Brother Newmark the Jew, a Greek refugee from Turkey, and myself the Gentile. So we were a scriptural trio: Jew, Gentile and Greek.

The Jew and the Greek slept in the same room. One night the Greek jumped up in the middle of the night and cried out: "I've got it!" He obviously did receive a mighty anointing from God. Brother Newmark felt that by getting very close to the Greek brother he would receive droppings too, but he did not receive any experience. God had met the Greek brother in a wonderful way and he now became a mighty prayer warrior, but I was uncertain whether he had actually received the Pentecostal baptism.

My hunger and thirsting for all the fullness of God had led me to devour every magazine I could lay hands on regarding these matters, and I was becoming convinced that they who received the scriptural Pentecostal baptism would speak with other tongues.

However, the devil did not leave me alone during this time. But my seeking the Lord was the most glorious time of my spiritual life. Prayer literally gripped my being. I would rise early in the morning and have a special season of prayer before breakfast. An amusing incident happened one morning. Since I felt that my pride was one of my

38 IMPOSSIBILITIES BECOME CHALLENGES

hindrances, I would confess what a wicked creature I was, confessing in my prayer times my tendencies toward the world and to sin. Unconsciously I did this in a loud voice so that even the neighbors heard it. Imagine my surprise one day when a European wrote me a letter saying he would have the police stop my praying if I persisted, saying that if he called me half of the names that I called myself in prayer, I would want to kill him.

A local church let us borrow its facility and we used it for prayer during the lunch hour, spending just a few minutes to eat our sandwiches and the rest of the time in prayer. We gave ourselves to intercession for souls and the various evangelistic workers with a real burden for revival. Again, in the evenings we were together in prayer. I also gave God the first hour in the morning for prayer for revival for Japan. At first I would awaken at twelve with an alarm clock and spend the first hour on my face before God. Later, the Lord Himself awoke me without an alarm and as I look back on those days, I know now that God was preparing me for a later ministry.

But I wondered why I did not receive the baptism. God had rigidly dealt with me and very definite restitution had been made along all lines. I had written letters of confession to many of my acquaintances that while I had appeared to be a good moral man, actually I was a religious hypocrite. I permitted the Lord to strip me along every line. Everything I did not feel absolutely necessary for living a respectable business life, or for the salvation of my own soul and of others, was given up, sold or given away. I was determined that there should be no hindrances to my receiving the baptism. Although my father did not accede to my wishes, I wrote asking him to burn all certificates obtained for my ability in shorthand or secretarial work.

I can never regret the amount of time it took to receive this glorious experience. Doubtless the devil did his best to interfere, for I soon found out that when I got to my knees the evil one would say to me "Do you not remember acting rather untruthfully today?" My tender conscience would agree that all had not been thoroughly above board and the

THE BAPTISM OF THE HOLY GHOST

devil then made me feel I had to live a perfect life first before I could receive God's gift. This is Satan's deception, for only on the merits of the blood of Jesus can we receive the gift of the Holy Ghost.

Finally the eventful day arrived! It was Monday evening, and one of the regular nights for prayer. At the all night prayer meeting the Saturday before, for the first time I felt that something definite had taken place in my spirit. While praying, I had felt that I was climbing and breaking through area after area, and the fear of man just went out and whatever anyone felt I did not care, I just bellowed out before God. Sunday morning I visited a Japanese church, and such a spirit of lightness was on me, it discouraged me, as I felt I had lost the stand of faith gained during the midnight hours Saturday. Returning home for a little rest in the afternoon, I walked into the meeting for Europeans that was being held at Brother Thornton's home. They had just gotten down on their knees for prayer. Immediately the spirit of faith gripped my soul again, and many thought I was receiving the baptism. Though I did not, it was fresh faith gripping my being.

The following evening (Monday), contrary to our usual custom, Sister Taylor had prepared quite a feast, a real good old English meal for us all. "You are weary. So much praying and fasting, you need to look after your physical", she said. I had no appetite for food. I wished to run to the hills and begin to lay hold of God. However, as a guest, I surrendered, and ate the first course. It was during the dessert that Sister Taylor began to read a tract that I had loaned her. It was entitled "Little is much if God is in it." While she read, I became more and more miserable. All the depths of my being were crying out to God for His Spirit. Surely God was faithful, and yet, what stone had I not turned to receive the Spirit? Every sacrifice possible had been made; even a personal typewriter had been sold and the proceeds given to God's work in my carefulness to have nothing stand between me and the baptism.

I felt so miserable and was under such conviction without the baptism that right then and there, while all

40   IMPOSSIBILITIES BECOME CHALLENGES

were eating their dessert (I believe it was apple pie and cake), I could have let go and cried out to God. Then I remembered that I was a guest in an English lady's home, and I pulled myself together to be proper. But only for a minute or so, for the conviction grew stronger, and at last I bowed my head and let the tears flow freely. I got down by the side of my chair and began to pray. My voice grew louder and louder. I determined to confess every sin over again. That finished, I pled every promise I could remember in the Bible. As far as I was concerned I had come to the cross-ways. It was to be a fight of faith to the death this time. When I started praying it was around eight o'clock, and I did not stop praying until somewhere around eleven thirty.

The feast was turned into a prayer meeting. Some got up and went home. The Greek brother going to another room received mighty intercession for me. He told me later that after some hours praying he received an assurance that God would meet my soul, so returning to the room where I was, the power came down upon me, he rejoicing as he heard me speaking in another tongue. Sister Taylor laid her hands on him, and he instantly fell backward and spoke in other tongues, glorifying God.

What I had gone through was a tremendous time of discouragement. As mentioned, I reconfessed every sin, pled again every promise, and by eleven thirty I had prayed out and lost my voice. There was not another word that I could say. Then the devil laughed at me, showed me how I had turned the feast into a prayer meeting, and how some had left wondering what kind of a fool I had made of myself. The devil showed me my tired body, lost voice, and teasing me said, "What have you got for it?" I certainly was discouraged.

Silently I waited on the floor, and had decided to go home, but just before going, in my heart I said: "Well, God, I will believe you anyhow." I could not even say this in a whisper, my voice had so gone. Just before getting up however, I noticed my little finger shaking. "There you are," the devil said, "You have prayed so hard, you are

THE BAPTISM OF THE HOLY GHOST

losing your balance." I willed to stop that finger shaking, but the more I tried to stop it the more it wig-wagged, and then I noticed a very definite feeling inside as of hot liquid. The prayer of David the psalmist came to me:

"Purge me with hyssop and I shall be clean."

God must be further preparing my heart, I considered, and began to praise Him some more.

I noticed that when I praised, the sense of hot liquid inside began to rise and rise. I also noticed that my voice began to return, and very soon I knew that whatever was inside had reached my throat. For a moment there was a halt, then a sort of struggle, and I remember dear Sister Taylor who had evidently been silently praying in the room, say in a whisper, "Lord, help him to go all the way."

Another moment, and like the rushing mighty streams of a flood, I was talking in other tongues. This lasted for about half an hour. Then the tongue changed, and again, another bursting through in a second language. This went on for about two hours, speaking in three different languages.

There was not the tremendous joy and exuberance I had expected at first. Rather there was a tremendous feeling of awe as I stood in the presence of God. I had seen the face of the King, and never again did I wish to open my eyes and look on the faces of human clay. To have to do so seemed to me a tragedy, but at one thirty in the morning I did open my eyes, got a little rest and went to the office as usual.

On the way I saw Brother Newmark, the Jew, going to his office coming in the opposite direction. He had returned earlier in the evening and had not heard what God had done to my soul. My inward feeling was "Oh, I wish he had received first. What shall I say to him as we pass?" As we met, I merely said "God was faithful last night, Herman." I had not been in the office five minutes before the telephone rang and he asked me whether I would spend that entire night in prayer with him for the baptism. "The change I saw in you as we passed this morning was so great that I dare not go to sleep another night until I receive the same experience," he said.

The experience of salvation was glorious. The manner in which God met me at the waters of baptism was wonderful. And the way in which I had daily fellowship with the Lord as I had obeyed Matthew 6:19 all defy description. But now what shall I say? My whole being was thoroughly transformed. I was literally walking on air. Praise, worship, and adoration was my every breath. Truly the experience can only be explained in scriptural language:

"Christ in you the hope of glory."

I had now become the habitation of God, and my body had become the temple of the Holy Spirit.

Although he had no way of finding out my experience, Brother Thornton saw me on my return from the office that day and immediately said, "Well, God has done something for you!" He could tell by the glow on my face. Some months after meeting a Christian businessman in a friend's home, he suddenly looked at me and said: "Brother Coote, you are so changed. What has happened?" I realized that this was our first meeting since I had been filled with the Holy Spirit, and he could see the difference!

Beloved reader, have you been baptized with the Holy Ghost? Have you received the flood of glory into your soul? The reality cannot be fully explained as it is actually heaven upon earth. Do not be afraid. Do not be misled by some fanatics, but go in for a scriptural infilling with God. He waits to baptize you with the fullness of His Spirit as He outpoured on the day of Pentecost. Yield to Him your all, believe all His Word, and receive all of it! It's glorious! It's glorious!

CHAPTER SIX

FIRST EVANGELISTIC EXPERIENCE

"Ye shall be witnesses unto me."
(Acts 1:8)

It soon became evident that I would have to make a clean cut from the world if I was to maintain my salvation and be aggressive for God. Foreign businessmen were expected to be members of one or more worldly clubs which included dances, theaters and general worldly social life.

Such conditions would soon have led to backsliding had not the Lord given me a passion for souls and shown me there were many spheres for using my leisure time working for God though still in business.

The first thing I did was to contact societies that printed gospel tracts. I investigated the publications of the Salvation Army, the Japan Book and Tract Society and the Oriental Missionary Society and ordered their Japanese tracts by the thousands with my name and address printed on them so those who received them could contact me for further spiritual help. At this time I traveled on the train to and from work and by going through the cars of the train, I could give out 500 tracts in one trip.

My bedroom became literally a tract depot, as in order to have enough tracts on hand, I had to order ahead. Every week postcards would be received from readers asking for more literature so I subscribed for 100 copies of a Japanese Christian newspaper and sent copies to those who requested more help. Any magazines I had left over, I would send to Japanese captains of ships that were docked at Kobe, as the newspapers reported the incoming vessels.

I then felt burdened for the neighbors of the district where I lived. Brother Thornton kindly loaned me a storehouse attached to the Missionary Home, and arranged with the Japan Evangelistic Band to send an evangelist to

44   IMPOSSIBILITIES BECOME CHALLENGES

help me twice a week.

Saturday afternoons were holidays from business, so with a bundle of tracts in my hand, I would visit every house in the neighborhood, inviting them to the meetings in the storehouse. Though I could not speak Japanese, I memorized a couple of sentences which I repeated at each house, parrot fashion. Some folks would think I spoke the language well, and I would stand there listening to them and nodding my head though not understanding a word that they said.

Not far from my house there was a large iron foundry where hundreds of men were employed. As the workers left for home on Saturdays at five o'clock, I would wait at the entrance giving out tracts. I had a large paper notice printed which I hung from my shoulder on which was advertised "Christian Newspaper, one sen," (a farthing), many of which I sold in a few minutes as the men left the factory.

It soon became evident that God was working in the neighborhood. A whole family: both parents, the grandmother and older children were all gloriously converted through the reading of a tract by the father. The head of a small factory was rescued from drink, and he in turn influenced his workers to find God. Soon I had to rent a building, and regular mission services were established.

Hundreds of souls heard the way of salvation, and many entered into an experience of saving grace. Drunkards, would be suicides and sinners of all descriptions made their way back to God through the cross.

But I was not satisfied. With the help of two other business friends, another mission was opened in the heart of Kobe, and here a greater saving work continued for some time. Then a convert of the first mission opened his home in a town to the right, and there a number of people sought the Lord. One night during street service a man who was deeply convicted came to the mission hall and came straight forward for salvation. He told me later that he had expected me to give him hard knocks on his head with my fist,

FIRST EVANGELISTIC EXPERIENCE

for he felt himself such a wretched sinner and deserved any punishment he could obtain. Today this man has opened his own work in northern Japan and is a successful pastor.

All this, though helping me grow in grace, had a contrary effect on the members of the firm where I worked. They felt I was disgracing myself and them by having street meetings with the banging of the drum as we do in Japan to gather the people. The train Europeans usually rode to the swimming pool in summer stopped right at the place where we had street meetings, and often I had to pray desperately as scorn and jeers would be hurled at me for taking my stand on the street and confessing Christ.

Some efforts were made to reach the Europeans in Kobe too, but the situation was exceedingly difficult. At first I had the fear of man in my heart. It was much easier on the trains to give out tracts to the Japanese. Many times when I got home I had to get down before God in repentance with tears because I had lacked the courage to give a tract to a European. But gradually God helped me to overcome this fear.

Now it is hard to believe that I had this trouble with the fear of man, for my tract distribution increased to an average of two thousand a day. Still, each morning I loaded my pockets with tracts in Japanese, English, German and French. Whenever a European would board the train I would put my hand in my pocket to give him one, but it seemed that hand became glued to the pocket. I could not pull it out. Though this fear paralyzed me time and again, I did not give up.

Each time I failed because of this fear, I would humble myself in repentance before the Lord and start out again. The next day the same failure might be repeated, but persistence in humbling and persevering prayer brought the victory. I can't say it ever became really easy, for the Europeans were not like the Japanese, and when they accepted the tract, it was like with a turned up nose, and then, to show me off before the Japanese passengers, they often would tear it up into small portions without ever

IMPOSSIBILITIES BECOME CHALLENGES

looking at it.

Actually, it was through handing a tract to a young Australian man that I was brought into contact with our Brother Newmark (the Jew), who was found by this Australian man at the club reading a New Testament.

During my later years in business I ate my lunch at a restaurant frequented by many Europeans and I would quietly pray in my heart as I entered for God to guide me as to where to sit in order for Him to give me the opportunity to give my testimony to someone. One day I was distinctly led to sit by another European, and I started talking about the war, hoping to turn the conversation to Christ. Finally my opportunity came. "What do you think of the outcome of the war?" he asked. Immediately I replied that I look at everything from a biblical standpoint, and shared with him how the Lord saved me through reading the Bible. He began to scoff, and during the remainder of the meal he mocked me so, I was glad when he paid his bill and left. But soon he returned, and throwing his name card over my shoulder he said, "Come see me sometime." I smiled, but committed the matter to God.

Time passed, and one day the conviction grew in me that I should visit him that night. I excused myself from my mission and went with the assurance that God was leading. The address was a local hotel, and I was familiar with the location, I thought. But to my amazement, I spent hours without finding it, and was about to return home when by chance I met Dr. Myers. "What are you doing here this time of the night?" he asked. I told him I was looking for the hotel, and he immediately directed me to it.

When I got there, the man was in bed. He put on his dressing gown, and we had a nice talk. Presently there was a knock on the door, and two others who had evidently overheard us in the next room, asked if they could come in and listen too. Now I had three: a Russian, an Australian and a Rumanian. The tables turned, and they began to force me to argue, and when I refused, they ridiculed me. Feeling I was wasting my time, I decided to leave, but

FIRST EVANGELISTIC EXPERIENCE

requested the permission to pray before doing so. This was granted, and I prayed like I would never see them again, asking God to help me pray before them as if they were dropping into a terrible hell. When I finished, the Australian took me aside and warned me to go slow cautioning me that I would soon be a lunatic if I did not take care. I merely replied that if he believed in hell fire as I did, he would be earnest too.

On the face of it, it seemed like the visit had been a failure, but at the office the next morning I found a two page typewritten letter from the Australian man, confessing that he could not sleep all that night because of deep conviction. He was a backslider who had lost touch with God through bemoaning the death of his only son in the war. He said he had ridiculed me to see if I were real or not. I met him again before his return to Australia, and as proof of his getting back to God he showed me various books for his own soul, he intended to read on board ship on his trip home, as well as many testaments and tracts he had bought to give out to the other passengers.

Another experience shows the wonderful way God led me to hungry souls. On a crowded street car one Saturday afternoon, not knowing there was another European on the car, I was asked: "What are you reading?" I was surprised to find a small Frenchman sitting next to me. When I told him it was the Bible and that I believed it all, and shared with him my testimony, he asked me if I would be willing to get off with him at the next stop. I agreed and he hailed a taxi. He drove me to his hotel and after going up to his room which he locked when we were inside, he told me his story. He was the son of a wealthy and prosperous businessman who had branches in New York, London, and Kobe. He had never had any inclination toward God as his life had been surrounded with material things. But he had been engaged to a young lady living in Shanghai, and just the week before he had received a cable stating that she had been shot dead through jealousy. The news so upset him he lost all interest in life. Try as he would, the club, the office, the hotel could not interest him any more and

IMPOSSIBILITIES BECOME CHALLENGES

everything seemed to mock him.

Discouraged and disgusted, he finally had decided to end it all and had bought a pistol, planning to end his life the next day at noon. How I prayed for guidance as he told his story! How wonderful that God had led me to travel by the same street car and sit down on the next seat to him, and that He had led me to read my Bible as we traveled! The next day, the man was to die by his own hands. I pointed him to Jesus and the Cross, and it was not long before the two of us were kneeling down seeking for his salvation. That day God caused this man to change his decision to end his life.

As I am writing this record many years after the above, I find it interesting indeed to recall some who definitely opposed my testimony in those days. There was one man, a little older than myself, who seemed to have a prosperous business and who lived not far from where I did. We often came in touch with each other. He could not stand me at any price, and my evangelistic efforts were a source of great pain to him. I remember on one occasion as we walked down opposite sides of the street his saying in a loud voice to a friend he was walking with, "I wonder why Coote does not take the drum with him to the office." I had to seek grace from the Lord to patiently bear this kind of continual opposition, but a sequel to it came when a few years ago I took a little rest and went to Tokyo to attend some special meetings held by the Salvation Army.

As I entered the meeting place, one of the older members of the Salvation Army staff greeted me with the words, "You are just the man I want. Come this way with me. I have had a real tussle with a European. I found him in a terribly filthy state, forsaken, and hungry. I have had him cleaned up, got someone to loan me a suit, and will have him to the meeting tonight. I want you to sit next door to him and see if you cannot get him to surrender to God." Naturally I wondered who the person could be. According to the description given to me, he must have been a desperate case. His face looked familiar, and during the meeting he spoke to me, saying "Say, have I not seen you

FIRST EVANGELISTIC EXPERIENCE

somewhere before? Did you ever live in Kobe?" Then I remembered that this was the man that laughed and scorned me; he was then in a prosperous business -- years had not been very kind to him. Wife, family, business, and friends were now all gone. Health, too, had departed, and now here he was without a penny and homeless. Even the clothes that he had on his back had to be borrowed a few hours previously, so he could appear in some sort of respectable fashion at the meeting.

How my mind went back to the different passages in the Psalms, especially in Psalm 37 which tells of the present boasting of the wicked as being empty. I refer to verse 30:

"I have seen the wicked in great power, and spreading himself like a green bay tree. Yet he passed away, and lo he was not; yea, I sought him, but he could not be found."

I am sorry to relate that this man still lives away from God. I have seen him several times when in Kobe on business and every time it is as a beggar pleading with me just to give him a few pennies so that he might get a cup of coffee. How true the Word of God is! In one respect only could it be said that I am like this man, in that I have nothing of this world's goods. Having yielded my all to the Lord, and believed His Word, I consider the various church buildings, and buildings on the Ikoma Bible College campus and buildings in San Antonio, Texas as proof that God is still the God of the Bible. Amen and Amen.

CHAPTER SEVEN

CALL AND SEPARATION FROM BUSINESS

*"A servant of Jesus Christ ... separated
unto the Gospel of God."
(Romans 1:1)*

Many circumstances combined together to prove that the firm that had employed me would send me home. In the first case I was an extra man, surplus and unnecessary to the office staff as the English headquarters of the firm had made a mistake in decoding a cable. Further, the Japan branch was making large annual losses and the European staff had to be cut down considerably. No less than twenty Europeans were sent home in two or three years' time. My aggressive activities for God, and the righteous stands taken in the office were disliked, so that whenever a reduction in the office was announced it just seemed to me to be miraculous that I was not one of the number to be sent home.

On more than one occasion conscience would not permit me to write down in the letter all that was dictated as I could not feel it was the entire truth. I merely left the parts out that I felt shady, explaining my stand, and requesting the managing director himself to write them in if he wished to stay with the original dictation.

On one occasion the managing director called me into his office, and enquired about my income tax, asking what figure I had turned into the authorities. I told him the exact amount that I received as salary. He explained my foolishness in doing so, and commanded me to rewrite my declaration stating a lower amount as my salary, as the inspector had called on him asking why it was that a member of his staff received a larger salary than the managing director himself. I had already fought a battle on my knees regarding the declaration of this income tax. The amount to be paid represented practically one month's salary out of

CALL AND SEPARATION FROM BUSINESS 51

twelve. I was supporting my parents in England, endeavoring to live as economically as possible, and sending the surplus in small amounts to various missionaries in Africa, Belgian Congo, China and India, besides supporting two or three missions in Japan. After I prayed I felt if I declared anything at all I should declare the full amount. I had to tell the managing director so and was determined not to move from my decision.

I really felt indebted to the Lord that He permitted me to be ministered to by some of His choice servants during my stay in Kobe. Some of the messages had very specially dealt with practical righteousness in Christians' lives. Restitution had played a very important part in my seeking the baptism of the Spirit. On one occasion after realizing that I had accepted extra expense money from my firm as well as samples of soap to which I had no right, when I turned in to the cashier what I felt I owed to the firm, others came under conviction and likewise paid for goods that they had expected to receive gratis. In seeking for revival in Japan I had read books written by Catherine Booth, the mother of the Salvation Army, and books on revival by Charles Finney in which he clearly points out the inconsistencies and pharisaic lives of professing Christians hindering revival in God's work.

While we are saved by grace and live by grace in this glorious grace dispensation, surely the grace of God should cause us to have a very tender conscience and make us to be thoroughly honest, not only with God but with our fellow man. Is it not true that much of the dullness of spirit among Christians, and the lack of power in the witness of believers is due to a carelessness along this very line? I remember eating at a restaurant one day when I was in a hurry. I had merely a simple lunch as I had very little time, and my bill amounted to 35 sen. I gave the cashier 50 sen and should have received 15 sen in change. Instead I received 20 sen; 05 too much. I did not want the extra five sen, but being in a hurry I did not bother about it and left the shop. I firmly believe the enemy so desired me to be careless in this matter that I might not have the authority in the Spirit to

52   IMPOSSIBILITIES BECOME CHALLENGES

deal with a battle that would occur soon, in other words by this little act of carelessness I was being robbed of my armour. I thank God He gave me grace to retrace my steps, confess that I had accepted five sen too much change, and return it, and my conscience was clear.

On another occasion, during the visit of special men from England when special reports had to be typed, and retyped by a certain date, instead of getting the reports corrected and ready for the final typing, the club was being frequented more than usual by the person responsible and it seemed evident to me that at the last minute I would be requested to work Sunday. This I was willing to do in an emergency, but when it could be avoided I did not feel willing to do so. I had a chat with the manager explaining my stand and telling him that I would work until Saturday midnight, and also from Monday morning at 1 o'clock, but that I wished my convictions about Sunday to be respected. He assured me there would not be any need for Sunday work, but my observations became true, and others at the last minute were asked to step in to type the reports on Sunday whereas I was free to obey my conscience, worship God, and preach in the open air and mission hall at night.

With the firm watching every opportunity to cut down expenses, reduce the staff, and send men home, it was a wonder of wonders that I was permitted to go on, and finish my business contract of five years.

I did not know that it was the will of the Lord for me to be a missionary in Japan until the business contract had been fully completed. One day the managing director called me for an interview regarding a new contract. He explained how the firm had been satisfied with me, and felt that I was the man to receive a better and higher position in the firm. He offered to make me perfectly satisfied regarding money matters if I would agree to a further period of service. I was not aware where the Lord would have me work for Him, but I felt the time had come to give up my business career, and use my time in seeking God, studying His Word, and preaching His gospel.

CALL AND SEPARATION FROM BUSINESS 53

I quietly informed the managing director of my decision and that I felt the Second Coming of Jesus was so near there was not time to be engaged in business from a money making standpoint, although I might be willing to work half days to pay for my living expenses.

I had a slight conviction that the Lord's will was for me to go to the Belgian Congo as a missionary. I had supported Brother Burton's work quite regularly and was considering the South African route home to England, stopping off at Durban and visiting the Belgian Congo for a period to see whether the Lord was really calling me to this field or not.

All arrangements had been made for leaving Japan; passage booked, bags packed, house given up and my successor employed in the office. Sister Taylor told me that God had spoken to her I was to be a missionary in Japan, but I was determined not to be influenced by anything anyone said, but get the direct witness from God Himself.

In order that God might speak to me I agreed to pray with this sister every morning of my last days at the office. Though this special time of prayer increased and deepened my assurance that God was working out His purposes for me, I still had no "Thus saith the Lord" regarding the matter.

My call came three days before the boat on which I was to sail for England, via South Africa, left the port of Kobe. It must be remembered that the firm had sought and obtained extra help in the office and so filled my position. The stand previously mentioned regarding finances of obeying Matthew, the sixth chapter, was strictly adhered to right to the very last. In fact more than this the Lord even began to teach me what a life of faith meant while I was still in business. During the last three months while I was there the printer of my tracts had made a mistake and I was faced with an invoice of almost double the amount that I had planned. Prayer was resorted to. See how wonderfully God answered prayer. A Christian traveller staying in Kobe a few days and wishing to give out tracts asked a friend of

IMPOSSIBILITIES BECOME CHALLENGES

mine where he might obtain them. The very day after I had prayed he came along, and after I had granted him his desires for the tracts gratis, he handed me 30.00 yen for the tract fund. Praise God from Whom all blessings flow.

Sensing in a measure that God was calling me to His service in some sphere or other and that possibly I would not be able to send help to my parents as I had done every month while I was in business, I had sent 50 per cent extra during the last twelve months. All in all God had blessed me, and yet as far as outward material blessings were concerned I had nothing, and the suit of clothes I was wearing was two years old.

I entered into the steamship office for my luggage labels and they said "We are sorry to tell you that we received a cable this morning stating that on account of the submarine danger in the Mediterranean Sea, sailings have been cancelled, and we cannot tell when we shall be able to issue tickets again." I was shocked and felt the hand of the Lord was moving in a special way. To make absolutely certain that this was God I went around to every other steamship office in town and when finally I realized that it was impossible to leave the country, I decided to have a special season of prayer and was on my way up to Sister Taylor's home when as clear as a distinct voice out of the skies I heard "Coote, Japan and Pentecost until Jesus comes." Right there and then I took off my hat, and accepted the will of the Lord for the remainder of my life.

I have described the joy that filled my soul when I was converted; the wonderful presence of His Spirit when I obeyed the Word and was baptized by immersion, and I have also spoken of the great assurance that came as I went through the books in my small library only permitting those to stay that would give testimony to Christ when He would come to catch His bride away. The victory won in Matthew 6:19, "Lay not up for yourselves treasures upon earth, where moth and rust doth corrupt, and where thieves break through and steal," had brought me into intimate fellowship with Christ, and the baptism of the Spirit had introduced me to the presence of God. But we are to go on from glory

CALL AND SEPARATION FROM BUSINESS 55

to glory. Amen. So with nothing, not even more than a few pennies of cash in my pocket, nothing in the bank, nothing in the way of household goods (I had already given away some blankets and what few household articles I had in preparation for going to South Africa) I was called to step out in naked faith. No one in the homeland could know what step I was taking. There was no possibility of obtaining even temporary employment in Japan to supply my daily needs. When the call came, there were no details as to how I was to obey, and yet though absolute foolishness from a business standpoint and seemingly welcoming disaster, I had not the slightest care, or worry as to how things were to come about. God had spoken, and if He had spoken, would He not work out every detail, and enable me to follow Him every step of the way?

Fifty years have passed. Many difficulties, temptations, discouragements and oppositions have been met, but I can truly say I have never doubted the call of God received on this particular day. At the time I received the call I was in a strange place financially. And writing this book fifty years later I can still say that I am in the same strange financial position. Without any salary, without any promise of support, mission board, committee, church, group of Christians, or any single individual I have scores of financial commitments to meet regularly in the way of mission rents, Bible School students' support, native workers' support, office workers' support, church expenses, printing of thousands of tracts, varied expenses for special evangelistic efforts, establishment of churches and building of permanent places of worship, besides the support of my own family, and my only foundation is the Word.

"Seek ye first the kingdom of God and His righteousness, and all these things shall be added unto you" (Matthew 6:20).

The day following the above mentioned call, I received a letter from a business acquaintance in Toronto, Canada, in which he told of a leading of the Lord to send me a check for $100.00, God thus confirming the stand I had taken to obey His call.

He mentioned how strange it seemed for him a business man sending an offering to another business man. It is quite possible that he may have thought that I was going to leave business and go into the ministry. Anyhow there had not been the slightest intimation on my part either by word of mouth or by letter that I had any leading in this direction and the brother continued that if he was wrong in his leading I was to use the money for the purchase of more tracts or give the offering into some Christian channel.

Another missionary gave me Yen 100.00 ($50) on the first day of my missionary career and I learned later that this represented all he had; God bidding him to empty his purse to do it.

Great is His faithfulness. "Impossibilities Become Challenges!"

ONE OF THE ORIGINAL TENT MEETINGS

CHAPTER EIGHT

FIRST OUTPOURING OF THE SPIRIT

"And they were all filled with the Holy Ghost,
and began to speak with other tongues,
as the Spirit gave them utterance."
(Acts 2:4)

The more I studied the question of the Pentecostal baptism from the naked Word, the more I was convicted that God's will for me was to be engaged in work that fully believed in the latter day outpouring of the Holy Ghost, with accompanying signs, as on the day of Pentecost.

When I was believing for this personal experience there were but a few Pentecostal missionaries in Japan, one or two in Kobe, and five or six in Tokyo, and one family in Yokohama. I had visited all of them, and had received a burden for the work, especially for the outpouring of the Spirit upon the Japanese by the time the Lord had called me out of business.

I had heard that possibly three individuals had at certain times received the baptism of the Spirit speaking with other tongues, but that Japan had not received a general outpouring. I myself, had great difficulty in praying the Japanese through to the baptism of the Spirit in the various mission halls that I had maintained while in Kobe, and I attribute a good deal of this to the absolute ignorance that I had regarding God's working along this line.

I remember once while still in business taking a prayer meeting in an upper room. My burden for the meeting was that the Christians should be baptized with the Spirit. After a couple of opening hymns, I read the last verses in Mark, exhorting them all to have a season of prayer, that God would honor His Word that very evening. As we went to prayer, God's power came down and I did not know it was God's power, I was so ignorant of the working of the Spirit.

IMPOSSIBILITIES BECOME CHALLENGES

Everybody who attended the meeting was mightily gripped by the power of God paying no attention to anyone, but all praying mightily together that God would honor His Word that very evening. After a few moments of prayer I felt they should stop praying; but they did not. I began to be afraid. I felt that they had gone beyond themselves, and could not stop. Finally, I tried to make them stop, by calling out the number of another hymn to sing and singing the hymn all the way through without one of them paying any attention to me; they were praying with all their might as I tried to call them down by my singing. I gave out the number of a second hymn, and sang that through without any better success. The devil whispered, "You have done it now; some of these have lost their mind." As I observed the situation more closely, I noticed that on the top of the stairs was a young man who had been knocked down by the power of God just as he reached the last step. Looking down the staircase there was another young man prostrated on the stairs praying earnestly, and still further just about to come up the stairs was a third in the same position.

I cannot help but smile at my ignorance as I consider this meeting. Truly this was a visitation from God. He was answering our prayers, and I did not know it, but was opposing it unconsciously. After unsuccessfully singing two hymns through to stop the believers praying, I had some of those who were not praying as earnestly to withdraw from the meeting, and I took them into another room, and gave them my message, leaving the rest praying as before.

It must be understood, however, that though this incident fully reveals how ignorant I was of the outpouring of the Spirit I had been convinced from the Word itself of the genuineness of the present day outpouring of the Holy Spirit, and was believing and expecting God to baptize the Japanese with the accompanying evidence of speaking with other tongues.

As I stepped out of business to become a missionary, two temptations confronted me to side track me from my God given conviction and revelation of Acts 2:4. I was invited one day to dine with a very successful and well known

FIRST OUTPOURING OF THE SPIRIT

missionary from China of the Christian Missionary Alliance. I was promised full fare to America, full privileges at the Nyack Bible School, and a position in their missionary work in South China.

Apart from my call to Japan, I merely mentioned that I believed one hundred per cent in Acts 2:4, and while I was told that the speaking in tongues was all right, I sensed right away that I would not be permitted to take a strong stand on speaking with other tongues, as on the day of Pentecost if I accepted the offer.

God hindered the other temptation from becoming a snare. Before taking the full stand that Acts 2:4 was a definite experience to be enjoyed by all Christians today, I was tremendously interested in the work of the Oriental Missionary Society, and had helped them considerably when the Lord permitted me to use my savings for missionary work. The late Brother Kilbourne grew interested in my decision to go all the way with God, and I, too, would have liked to have joined this society, but again the question of Acts 2:4 was considered by them as not God's plan for this dispensation. This closed the door, and threw me back on God.

When the call "Japan & Pentecost until Jesus Comes" was given to me at the close of my business contract I felt a strong leading to go to Yokohama, and help Brother and Sister Gray. At that time they had a work in Ibaraki Ken, chiefly centered in the town of Koga, but were in charge of a mission in Yokohama during the furlough of another missionary. Sister Gray was far from well, and was not able to go to the meetings. Brother Gray had not then received the baptism, which hindered him from aggressive work, so that my coming to help them was greatly appreciated.

One of my first requests perhaps rather shocked them. I asked permission to hold AN EVERY NIGHT CAMPAIGN UNTIL THE POWER FELL. I was so definite in my stand that my request meant that no matter what happened I was determined to carry on until the power fell upon the work at Yokohama as it did on the day of Pentecost.

I seemed to feel an inward voice telling me not to bother with the Japanese language study at that time or to open up my own work but to give myself to prayer, and to the minute study of the Acts of the Apostles during the day, and also battle through in prayer to an outpouring of the Spirit on the Japanese people.

I had an old blanket, and forming a daily program for myself, I usually left about ten in the morning for the hills, returning at noon, and doing the same thing at two in the afternoon, returning at four, spending these hours in intercessory prayer or simply waiting on God in silence and reading and rereading the Acts of the Apostles.

The nightly meetings commenced with real enthusiasm. I was a new missionary to the Christians, and all promised success. But after the first week, and every message bearing on the same subject "Be ye filled with the Spirit," some of the Christians began to grow tired; others wondered what I was driving at, and the attendance was not as good during the second week.

I kept on, two weeks, three weeks, simply trusting God for an outpouring of the Spirit, and determined to carry on until it came. Regularly the hills found me waiting on God. My spot was where few, if any, came in the day time, so I had glorious times of fellowship in prayer and communion with God. Once or twice, however, wood cutters found me, and would arouse me, asking me if I was sick or something. My faith aimed at a mighty outpouring of the Spirit in which hundreds would receive, but the second and third weeks quickly convinced me that I had challenged the devil to a regular conflict. The crowds in the evening services dwindled; Christians put their heads on one side, and queried my methods. The more earnest seekers grew tired and no one received the baptism.

Doubts invaded my prayer tabernacle in the hills. Would I have to give up? The third week; fifth and sixth weeks were no better. Rather the reverse. Numbers in the evening service dwindled down to twos and threes, and one

FIRST OUTPOURING OF THE SPIRIT

night my interpreter failed to appear. But while my faith was tested I did not give up. I finally believed God for just three to receive the baptism. This was a terrible come down from my early stand for hundreds to receive the Spirit.

But I kept on praying day after day, and going to the hills waiting on God and trusting Him for the guidance to bring Holy Ghost power. Only rain prevented me from my daily prayer visits. I remember once laying my blanket on several inches of snow and just waiting before God.

It was the seventh or eighth week when God began to move, just at the time when things looked the blackest. The attendance had dwindled down to nothing; the workers had considered me extreme, and the Christians themselves had begun to lose faith in me. One night three men came into a spirit of laughter. There was no baptism, but the laughter was undoubtedly supernatural. As I observed these three young men laughing in the Spirit, my faith rose, and inwardly I said "Lord, I will now believe for ten to receive the baptism."

The morning following these same three young men came to the home of Brother and Sister Gray greatly burdened. They told how they had not been able to sleep during the night. God who had been faithfully working had allowed them to have some sort of revelation in the Spirit, and through this they had come to know the awfulness of their sin. One of them had deceived his father, by unlawfully using his father's seal, and had cheated in the sale of cattle. Confessions were made, hearts were humbled and it was evident that a break was at hand.

In two or three more days as one of these same men was kneeling at his chair in the mission he sweetly spoke with other tongues and glorified God. Others were now influenced to go to the altar, and the Spirit of God began moving upon the people. My faith jumped, "Lord I will now trust for twenty-five to receive the baptism." It was not long before two or three more received and spoke with other tongues. The altar meetings increased in numbers, and in

62   IMPOSSIBILITIES BECOME CHALLENGES

length. Soon, as many as twenty and twenty-five would be at the altar from the night meeting to the early hours of the morning.

Three, five, seven, ten received the Spirit. Again my faith jumped, and I said "Lord, I now believe for one hundred to receive the Spirit." Though God had wonderfully honored His Word, and answered prayer, the battle was still an uphill fight. Apart from Sister Gray's Bible woman who had received the Spirit, no worker had yet received the baptism. Unless they did, success for Pentecost in Japan could not come. I was conducting the meetings through an interpreter who was opposed to speaking in other tongues. The mission itself was the property of one on furlough whose interpreter had not received the baptism. Brother and Sister Gray who were temporarily in charge had a worker who felt he had received the Spirit without speaking with other tongues. But God was faithful. The New Year came, and a sort of convention was held at which six or seven native workers were present. It is interesting to see how some of them received the Spirit. I knew that my own interpreter was opposing me. He was a man who could be called my double. About the same age, the same height, and he had been converted in Kobe about the same time as I. He was a good interpreter, and we worked well together, but he could not take the Acts 2:4 stand. However, night after night, it was the same message, followed by the same kind of prayer meetings. Souls were stirred, some weeping, were prostrated, and some were speaking with other tongues. It became evident that sooner or later he would have to fall in with the situation, or fall out.

My burden at the hill prayer seasons was now for individual workers. I remember how the Lord led about my interpreter. Daily I brought him to the throne of grace in faith that God would break through and then one day I found that I could not pray any further. My mouth was stopped. Feeling perhaps the enemy was opposing, I forced myself to pray, but could not, and so yielded to whatever God was doing.

FIRST OUTPOURING OF THE SPIRIT

I noticed nothing unusual in the night meeting, until the altar service. I wondered where my interpreter was, as I could not find him. Perhaps he has gone home, I thought, as I knew he was indifferent to these seasons of prayer, but suddenly I saw a sight, and I truly wondered whether I was dreaming or not. There at the end of the line of seekers was my interpreter, his hands raised, his face lit up with the light of heaven, and he was praising the Lord at the top of his voice in other tongues.

Oh glory, I thought inwardly, what has happened? I said nothing, but later he informed me that during the day while sitting in his own home reflecting on the services, he knew he had come to the crossroads. Either he would have to break the relationship with me, or go for the baptism, with all his heart. He realized he could not go on the way he was. Two could not walk together unless they were agreed.

He said he left his home and went to the hills, not far from where I was praying. He knelt down on the ground and said, "Lord, I offer myself without any reserve, a full and complete surrender," and immediately the power of God struck him. He fell over into a hole that was near him, and in that position he received the baptism, spoke with other tongues, and glorified God. Praise the Lord.

Brother Gray's chief worker who had so resolutely felt he did not need the Pentecostal experience began to visit the hills, too. One day when we were sitting down to lunch he entered the dining room, raised his hands, closed his eyes, and poured out his heart in continuous praises to God, speaking with other tongues. This was about the most literal fulfillment of living water flowing from anyone's inward being that I have ever witnessed. One could almost see the billows and the waves, as well as the rushing currents of praise ascending up to the throne of God. Praise God from whom all blessings flow.

The meetings continued night after night. The news had spread among the Christians and those who had felt strange toward me now began to come back. One prominent member who had stayed away came back, and sat on the

64 IMPOSSIBILITIES BECOME CHALLENGES

back seat; the next night she sat half way up the aisle, the third night she knelt down in the aisle, and tears began to flow. The following evening she was at the altar, her hands raised, and the power of God causing her body to shake.

The district became a little stirred. Not because of the preaching, for open air work had been temporarily stopped. But the combined sound of the praises of God's people nightly, caused the crowds to come and peep in. We could not let the crowds satisfy their curiosity, so we locked the doors during the waiting periods. The people outside climbed up at the windows, got on the roof, and tried in every way possible to find out what was going on inside.

One night the police compelled the doors to be left unlocked, and six or seven policemen came in to investigate. God arranged the matter so nicely that the seekers had all gotten settled on their knees at the altar before they appeared, and the police left before the meeting was over, so that their presence did not disturb the seekers.

They looked around the room, looked into what Bibles, or hymn books they could find on the seats, searching evidently for some kind of explanation for what was going on at the altar. One policeman did not like the falling under the power of God, so he came forward and politely placed one of the young women who had fallen under the power on her knees again. Immediately she went over again, and a second time he placed her on her knees. This was repeated several times, and each time she fell backwards under the Spirit. Finally, he became disgusted, called out "baka" (fool) and left the meeting.

One of the young seekers would always stand up, while he was praising the Lord. The power would come down on him, and he would sway backwards and forwards. Without bending his knees, and with his whole body stiff, he would fall backward. At first I felt sure he would hurt himself, but as this happened every night, I realized the Holy Spirit was leading, and that God knew His business. One evening as this happened he fell and struck the rung of a chair, which ordinarily would have dislocated his neck, and could have

FIRST OUTPOURING OF THE SPIRIT

caused his death. Later when I asked him how he felt, he was surprised to think that I thought he might be hurt. He was unaware of falling and had no pain.

One of the most remarkable cases of God's supernatural working was that of a poor, outcast ignorant young woman. Brother and Sister Gray had trouble getting help in the home. As Sister Gray taught the Bible in the mornings, had night meetings, and had many home duties, she cried to God that He would send someone to help her. That very day, this girl came. Whether God had another purpose in sending her to the missionary home, either to teach us all patience or not is another matter!

One night during the altar service a peculiar scream was heard from the back of the hall. Wondering what it was, I was told that this girl was taken seriously sick, and permission was asked to call for the doctor. I refused, saying that God with His power was there to heal and to meet every need.

The next morning she confessed to us that she was not sick, but she made this as an excuse for her screaming. She was a harlot born to a harlot. The real trouble was that the power of God had ferreted out her awful sins, and she could not stand the conviction. Practically the whole day was spent listening to her confessions, which were many, but finally she seemed to come to some sort of peace in God. When she was baptized in the Spirit, she went into a sort of trance. She could not read a line in the Japanese Bible so was unable to commit scriptures to memory.

But nightly as she came under the power of God in the services, she quoted long portions of scripture from the books of Revelation, Job and Isaiah. Not only would she quote these books but she would act out the scenes with her body movements. It became a regular habit for my interpreter and I, as she came under the Spirit of God, to get our Bibles and check her words and actions with the scriptures. We stood amazed before the power of God. We were having the power of God demonstrated right before our very eyes. Well do I remember when she acted the eighteenth chapter of Revelation, and to this day the effect it had upon my own soul, as she with strong cryings and tears called out in the Spirit, "Babylon the great is fallen, is fallen."

But one night I was tempted to believe there was something wrong. In quoting a chapter from the book of Revelation, and I mean whole chapters, she used a word that was different to both Japanese and English versions. That night I returned home a little puzzled, but as it was a hot evening I did not immediately retire, but laid on the bed with my clothes on, meditating. It came to me to look up the particular place in the Revised American Bible, and to my delight I found that what I had thought was a mistake, i.e., the word used by this girl when under the power of the Spirit, was actually the correct word given in the Revised American Version. This confirmed to my own soul in a truly wonderful way the fact that God was showing forth His marvelous acts in this ignorant girl.

Allow me to definitely emphasize the fact that there was absolutely no possibility in any way whatsoever of the girl knowing that the word in the Japanese and English versions was different to that of the American version, for the girl herself could not even read a verse of scripture in the Japanese Bible, much less any knowledge of English.

Rejoice, and again I say- Rejoice!

CHAPTER NINE

THE OUTPOURING SPREADS TO OTHER CITIES

"Ye shall be witnesses unto me both in Jerusalem,
and in all Judea, and in Samaria, and unto
the uttermost part of the earth."
(Acts 1:8)

Yokohama had become the Jerusalem of the outpouring of the Spirit, and as the missionaries residing in the towns of Tokyo and Kobe had heard of the outpouring, requests began to come in for special meetings to be held with them too.

Our first meetings were out in the country. This country work had been opened through the conversion of a drunken milkman in Yokohama whose older sister had been baptized with the Holy Ghost and had gathered together a group of elderly people, and with her little knowledge of God, she told them to raise their hands and praise the Lord, and God would bless them. She wrote to us for meetings, and we felt it good to have a few days rest from the work in Yokohama and hold these special meetings in the country.

The record of these meetings may sound like fiction, but praise the Lord, every word that I use to describe them indicates not half of what took place. The location was quite a distance from the railway depot so that we had to walk a good deal, and we arrived in time for a small evening meeting in a farmhouse. There were sixteen people gathered together, practically all past middle age, which rather disturbed me. As I saw their blackened teeth, a sign of widowhood, and realized how little they knew of the elementary principles of the Gospel, I felt helpless to bring them in touch with God. Besides this I was still using an interpreter which added to the difficulties of the situation.

However, I had decided to just teach the old folks that evening one or two simple Gospel songs, and the following evening tell them a little more about the great Gospel. This

68 IMPOSSIBILITIES BECOME CHALLENGES

was my decision as I opened Brother and Sister Gray's baby organ, and looked through the song book for a simple suitable hymn. Before starting to play, however, I looked up and was astonished at what I saw. Two or three of the folks who had gathered and were waiting in a circle had their eyes closed; their hands raised, praising Jesus and their bodies quivering under the power of God.

My spontaneous "Hallelujah" caused others to praise the Lord, and before I knew it, as many as thirteen were on their backs prostrated by the power of God; one large woman being thrown bodily across the room, and that night without any preaching, in fact the meeting was never opened, three or four received the baptism of the Holy Spirit, and spoke with other tongues glorifying the Lord.

How amazed I was! Although I had seen the mighty works of God in Yokohama, unbelief had still gripped me, for I had decided in my heart that these ignorant old folks would not understand the things of God, and inwardly I had postponed giving them the message until the following evening deciding to merely teach them one or two simple Gospel songs.

Hallelujah! I feel like shouting it a thousand times over! Oh what would happen if a man believed God? This is what happened when a man did not believe God. What would happen if we truly believed the Lord?

The next morning I did not awaken as early as the others. Many of them slept in the same farmhouse with myself, and my workers. The Japanese are very enthusiastic about closing tightly all windows and doors at night, being afraid of the night air, and so with merely a bed on the floor, and a pillow almost as hard as wood, I did not awaken as early as usual.

When I did awaken, however, I heard something going on in the next room. As I peeped through the paper sliding doors, I saw a sight that went right to my heart. One of the old folks who was in the meeting the night before had not come under the power of the Spirit. He was around 65 years of age and had a fine white flowing beard which gave

THE OUTPOURING SPREADS TO OTHER CITIES   69

him quite a dignified appearance.

He was now earnestly discussing the question as to
whether the blood of Jesus Christ really cleansed a man
from all sins. Over and over he would say to my worker
across the Japanese table, "But are you sure the blood
cleanses from all sin?" The worker would open the Bible
and show him in black and white where we are told if we
confess our sins, God is faithful and just to forgive us and to
cleanse us from all unrighteousness. But somehow the old
man could not be influenced to believe it right away. He
wished to be positively sure and for some time he did not
grip the truth. Then suddenly I noticed a smile creep across
his countenance, his hands began to rise, and then he
shouted "banzai", (hurrah), and in the Japanese language,
"Yes I believe the blood of Jesus does cleanse from all sins."
I noticed his raised hand quiver, his body begin to sway, and
in a very short time, he, too, was prostrated under the
power of God, and within five minutes he was speaking with
other tongues, and praising the Lord, having received the
baptism of the Holy Ghost.

I felt God had performed a wonderful miracle in this
old gentleman. But I realized this fact more so a few days
later when the meetings were transferred to his village.
They were again held in a farmhouse; but the people who
gathered together were totally different. This time it was
mostly young people who crowded into that farmhouse, and
they were laughing and joking during the earlier part of the
service. I was a little disturbed, for I thought nothing much
could happen with such lightness going on.

Just as I started to speak, the white haired old
gentleman who had received such a wonderful experience
in the former village approached me and in a whisper said,
"This is my village. I have lived here many years. May I give
my testimony?" I was glad for him to do so, as I did not feel
the meeting was yet in a right mood for the message. He
got down on his knees, Japanese fashion, and in a very slow,
dignified, and reverent manner told how he was known to
them all; had lived in their village well over 50 years, but
that there was one thing that had bothered him terribly for

IMPOSSIBILITIES BECOME CHALLENGES

at least 49 years. He explained in much detail what this point was. He told how as a young man he had a very bad temper, and had two particular enemies in the village that he often quarrelled with. His enmity against them was such that he desired to murder them, and the opportunity to do so came.

He disposed of their bodies by placing them in a sack after killing them, and the matter of their death had remained a secret. He told how after murdering them his conscience bothered him. Always when he went to bed at night he could imagine the eyes of the murdered men following him around the room, and even in the daytime he seemed to be haunted by their spirits. He had tried in various ways to obtain relief for his conscience by religious methods, but had always failed. Then he told of the meeting in the former village how he felt the power of God, and yet was not fully convinced until the following day he felt the power of God upon his own body, and had an inward witness that the blood of Jesus had cleansed him from all sins.

He told his story in a reverent manner, and was soon crying tears of deep repentance before his village neighbors. The same spirit of weeping and of repentance gripped the meeting, and practically everybody in the room was broken up and crying. We were unable to have the regular message, but we went in between the praying and crying people exhorting them to look to the Cross, and to Jesus, Who died for their sins.

I do not believe I have witnessed such a spirit of repentance and of weeping over sin as I witnessed that night. As already mentioned it was impossible to preach, for some were in deep agony, and were literally crying aloud for deliverance and salvation.

The next day the village policeman came to see me, and referred to the previous evening's meeting. He rather surprised me by the statement that I had gotten him into trouble. I did not know just what he meant. But he explained by saying that while he was returning from his

THE OUTPOURING SPREADS TO OTHER CITIES   71

regular beat the previous evening when still a number of blocks away from where we were holding the meeting he could hear strange sounds.

He actually said that at first it sounded to him like cattle about to be slaughtered. As he approached the place, however, he realized that they were people, and he felt he must make a report of the meeting to his superior officer. But he expressed his difficulty by saying that he did not know how to make out the report, and did not wish to show any opposition to Christianity, but had to make a report, so had a request to make.

He said, "Will you, Mr. Coote, practice mesmerism tonight, the same as you did last night, making the people to scream and cry, and I will be present with pencil and notebook to make remarks?" I very earnestly told him that there was nothing of mesmerism about the meeting and that the reason the people were in agony and crying was that the Spirit of God had shown to them their sins. I, myself, had nothing whatsoever to do with it, not having preached.

We had wonderful times in this second village. Many prayed right through to salvation; were baptized in water and baptized in the Holy Ghost and spoke with other tongues.

One afternoon, a very dignified, tall, seemingly wealthy man came to see me. He explained he had not been to the meetings but quite a number of his household, including his farm laborers had. After chatting about a number of matters for quite a long time, he said he had come to ask me a question. It was whether I would explain to him the meaning of a word he heard members of his household use in their conversations regarding our meetings. He had to stop and think a few moments before he could himself remember the word. Then he said "I have it. The word sounds something like 'Jesus'." Continuing, he said, "What is Jesus? Is it the name of something you are selling or advertising? Just what is Jesus? I rather imagine" he said, "that it must be the name of a soap you are selling, for whenever I hear the word used it is done so in connection with washing and cleansing."

The impression made by his remark on my soul will never be forgotten. Imagine, a man of wealth in middle age, living only twenty or thirty miles from Tokyo, the capital of Japan, not knowing the name of Jesus; wondering whether it was the name of an article that I had for sale. Should not this incident bring us to our knees and help us afresh to consider the Great Commission given by our Lord to His Church?

MEETINGS IN TOKYO

Brother and Sister Juergenson had given me a hearty welcome to conduct special meetings for their converts in Tokyo. They had at that time two churches, and they gathered the converts into one place and arranged a special week's meetings that they might be baptized with the Holy Ghost. The first night after talking to the Christians on the baptism, I felt the Spirit distinctly bid me not to have an altar call, but to close the meeting with a word of prayer. This I did, and the second night God granted liberty for an altar call for those who wished to receive the Spirit. One young man told us that after the first meeting he could hardly sleep for thinking on the meaning of the words "Holy Spirit," and it was truly wonderful on the second night as I called them to the altar. Several young men came forward and knelt down on their knees. Before allowing them to pray, I exhorted them very definitely to be sure of their standing before God - all sins forgiven - lives fully surrendered to God and to His will - as well as a distinct faith that God would baptize with the Holy Ghost.

When each one of the seekers had given me the assurance that these things were all right in their lives, I said "Now raise your hand, just worship the Lord, and soon the power will fall." I had hardly gotten the words out of my mouth when just as if they had all been shot down by the same bullet from the same gun they were all thrown down

THE OUTPOURING SPREADS TO OTHER CITIES   73

by the power of God, and one or two received the baptism of the Spirit that night, several others receiving later in the week.

After this week of special meetings a whole month of evangelistic meetings was also held, and some of the most wonderful baptismal services that I have ever witnessed were held at this time. The power of God came down on the seekers shaking under the power of God in the water, and on several occasions they had to be assisted on the return journey as they were not able to walk alone because of the power of God upon them.

POWER FALLS IN KOBE

I was not invited to hold special meetings in Kobe, but I had to go there on business. I visited dear Sister Taylor, and told her and some of the folks who were in her home of the wonderful things that God was doing in Yokohama, and Tokyo, as well as in the villages. That impromptu visit turned into a seeking meeting, one of the Japanese workers being struck by the power of God; an Englishman was prostrated under the power, later speaking with other tongues, and the brother of the Greek refugee also receiving the baptism of the Spirit.

WORK AMONG UNIVERSITY STUDENTS

Sister Bernauer of Tokyo was very anxious that I would have some meetings for her. Her work was on rather a different order to the other missions, but nevertheless blessed of God. She lived close to the universities, helping students with English, and they would come to the Sunday services. Quite a number had been baptized in water, and Sister Bernauer's wish was that they should be baptized in the Holy Ghost.   After the first meeting, these university students objected to the free praise and worship. They absented themselves from the second night's meeting, some writing letters saying they were not going to have that kind of a meeting. This disturbed both Sister Bernauer and myself, but I knew prayer was the only refuge.

I confessed my lack of wisdom etc. to God, and by the time for the commencement of the third meeting God had caused these students to open their Bibles and read in places where different ones prayed with a loud voice and glorified God. Before the week was finished all of them had returned, and the power came down upon them, and they too, were praising the Lord with loud voices, and speaking with other tongues.

I cannot leave this chapter without adding a remark or so on the wonderful way that God honored every attempt at unity among the workers. While these different missionaries were Pentecostal, and were praying and believing for an outpouring of the Holy Ghost on the Japanese, there were differences of opinion held on some minor points of doctrine. I was asked once when starting special meetings what I believed. I was rather taken aback. I had been under the impression that all Spirit filled people believed alike, but soon found out that this was not so. Some believed in three distinct works of grace; others in but two and again there were some who believed in just one. I was asked how many I believed in. Facing the question suddenly, I had to reply "I do not know." But continued that I would bring the matter to God, and give my reply the next day. While praying about this point, God gave me the following answer: (1) The blood of Jesus Christ to cleanse from all sins; (2) The baptism of the Holy Ghost as recorded in Acts 2:4; (3) The Second Coming of Jesus Christ; (4) The necessity of a holy life. These points were acceptable to the missionaries of the various branches of Pentecost so that God was able to grant me the privilege of combining my efforts and prayers with the various missionaries in Kobe, Osaka, Tokyo, Yokohama, Hachioji and Tachikawa.

One Norwegian missionary who had not been in Japan long, however, did not feel that he could permit me to come and help him. He contended that some slight difference between us was sufficient reason for his not

THE OUTPOURING SPREADS TO OTHER CITIES 75

asking me to come and help; and yet he wished to see his converts baptized with the Holy Ghost. He finally approached me, and I gave him full assurance, that on points where we differed there would be the fullest ministerial courtesy shown. He asked me for four days. Nothing special took place the first two, but God's power came the third, and on the fourth the meeting was so free and easy that we went from one to another laying on hands and the power came immediately upon the Christians, and they received the baptism of the Spirit, speaking with other tongues.

POWER FALLS AT HACHIOJI

Miss Dithridge, a former Baptist missionary who had received the baptism of the Spirit during a time of furlough in America had returned and started work here in Hachioji, but was quite concerned because none of her converts had received the baptism. As I had not felt led to associate myself with any of the existing branches of Pentecost, feeling that God had enabled me to stand alone before Him she felt a little disturbed whether she would be right or otherwise in inviting me to take some meetings. God, however, arranged that we should meet in Karuizawa and special meetings were arranged. During that week practically every one of her converts received the baptism, and they were days of heaven on earth.

Sing unto the Lord a new song!

CHAPTER TEN

MARRIAGE

"And both Jesus was called, and his
disciples, to the marriage."
(John 2:2)

After my conversion, well meaning friends tried to influence me to get married. They even pointed out some whom they thought would be good life mates, but in God's own peculiar way He made me to know that this was a matter for Him to settle. I had an inward conviction that marriage was one of the most important steps in a Christian's life. Marriage could either lead a Christian down to failure, or be a mighty help in God's hand to greater successes.

For these reasons then I vowed to God that I would never seek marriage. I wish to make myself clear. I did not say I would not marry, but rather would not seek marriage. I really felt that I would be married, but was perfectly willing to leave the entire matter to God, and to trust Him fully to lead in every detail.

My first conviction from God that it would be a blessing for me to be married came when the Spirit was first outpoured in Yokohama. Night after night seekers would remain before God until the early hours of the morning. As the men folks had to go to work they were not able to seek as late as the women folks; therefore I often found myself alone with a number of women seekers. For appearance sake, at any rate, it was advisable that I be married.

God had led Miss Esther Ione Keene to leave her American home for Japan as a missionary. She felt led to help Mrs. Taylor in her rescue work in Kobe. I had met her on my visit to Kobe, and noted her earnestness for God, her keenness for holiness and her separation from the things of the world. I little realized, however, she was God's choice

MARRIAGE 77

for my life's partner.

Correspondence had passed between us regarding doctrinal points surrounding Acts 2:4 and Acts 2:38, and I had been experiencing some very keen financial testings, but these were unknown to anybody. Just when I did not have more than a few coppers left, a letter would come from Sister Keene containing her tithe. This happened several times until I wondered whether I was not allowing the enemy to bring my feet into a snare. But after much prayer I had the deep conviction that Esther Keene was God's choice for my life, and finally the Lord led me to write her explaining the whole situation. The letter was returned without being received. I sent it off again believing that if it came back a second time it would be a proof that I was entirely out of order and had not the mind of the Lord.

Instead of the letter coming back a second time, I received Sister Keene's reply after she had fasted three days and three nights over the matter. We both felt the matter to be clearly from the Lord and the wedding day in October was fixed.

Up to this time I had been living with my Japanese married worker. I had two small rooms upstairs, furniture consisting of a small bed, an old desk, and one or two old chairs. I ate Japanese food three times a day, sitting on the floor, using chopsticks with the Japanese worker's family. Marriage therefore meant renting another house and buying proper furniture, which would involve a considerable sum of money.

No one in the homeland in connection with Pentecostal or Full Gospel work had ever met me, as I had started missionary life right from the day my business contract ended without leaving Japan. God had very graciously supplied my needs, and I rather expected a considerable sum to come in for the wedding, and renting of the home, etc., especially as God had so wonderfully led in the matter.

But I was disappointed. I did not receive any greater financial help than usual. I was really in a predicament, for in Japan it is customary when renting a house to pay down what is known as "shikikin." This is a sort of guarantee money, generally equivalent to three month's rent, which is deposited with the landlord who holds the same until you give up the house. In some cities, like Osaka, the landlord will even deduct from this deposit money a certain amount, if the term of renting is less than one year, and for depreciation.

I not only had no deposit money, but nothing for the rent, and no furniture to put in the house. But God never fails the trusting soul. He will ever make the iron to swim.

My Japanese worker lived at Sugamo in the suburbs of Tokyo, and I was at the same time looking after Brother and Sister Gray's work at Kogamachi in Ibaragi Prefecture. It came to me one day to visit the city of Omiya which is just half way between the two points, and see if I could not find a tiny house of some kind that I could rent at little or no expense. My thought was really contrary to reason for this deposit money and rent in advance is a very strict rule in Japan.

Wandering around Omiya I met a foreign lady. She was an Episcopal missionary, and she thought I was possibly looking for her. However she invited me to a cup of tea, of which I gratefully partook. When I casually told my errand she exclaimed, "God sent you," and I was quite surprised for we were utter strangers to each other.

Her explanation was that she had built her house, and had to leave for England. She did not wish to rent the house during her absence, but had been praying for a European who would be willing to live in it and take care of it. She was leaving one or two of her workers in one part of the house, and granted to me the complete use of three bedrooms, sitting room, and kitchen, etc. The home was nicely furnished, and we had the use of these for almost a year for just a mere trifle every month. This was a genuine miracle, and supplied our housing needs in a wonderful way.

But though God had so graciously undertaken for the housing question, unbelief teased me every day regarding

MARRIAGE   79

the question of clothes. I could not possibly be married in the one shabby suit that I then possessed. And yet no funds came in, and the time for the wedding was right at hand. But God is never late. I distinctly remember His leading me to a second hand clothing shop in Yokohama and bringing my attention to a dead man's suit. It fit me just as if it had been made for me. I had it sent to the cleaner's right away, and folks admired my wedding suit, but some were shocked when they were told that it was a dead man's suit. You may not approve of this, a dead man's suit to be used on one's wedding day, but God knows how to get the starch out of our natures. A large gift of money at that time might have fed my pride, while the dead man's suit helped me to strengthen my stand in giving God a full and complete surrender.

Even my wife did not know where I got the suit until after the wedding day, and then what do you think I found out? Well, that her wedding dress had been bought in America months before, second hand, for just $1.00. Praise the Lord.

LEONARD AND ESTHER COOTE

CHAPTER ELEVEN

MIRACULOUS SUPPLY OF NEEDS

*"Seek ye first the kingdom of God, and His
righteousness: and all these things
shall be added unto you."
(Matthew 6:33)*

In detailing incidents in which God miraculously supplied needs for every day living, may it be remembered that I had never visited any Pentecostal assembly in the homeland, having become acquainted with Pentecostal work while living in Japan, and stepping right out of business without any visible means of support as a faith missionary, while maintaining a distinct Pentecostal testimony.

It is natural then to report that my treasury was invariably empty. God had given me a good start on leaving my employment by allowing a business acquaintance to send $100.00 from Toronto a month beforehand, as well as leading a Japanese missionary to give me his last 100 Yen. Later, the business firm for which I had worked granted me three months salary in lieu of return fare to England. This, however, I turned over to God as a special account to use, so that while I was myself living a life of faith I might also have the privilege of continuing to be a steward of God's work in other places and countries.

The first time that I remember a definite need being met in a surprising way was one evening when there was no meeting. The month was drawing dangerously near to the end when rents and other expenses had to be met, and there was not sufficient in hand to meet the needs. Alone in my room I was waiting before God, presenting the various needs, and showing to God the depleted treasury. As I prayed, I believed God, and a consciousness God was faithful came over my being, and I finished praying assured that everything would be allright.

MIRACULOUS SUPPLY OF NEEDS 81

As I arose I was astonished to see on the floor beside me four letters, all from America. As I was praying and waiting before the Lord my interpreter had come into the room and laid the letters by my side, but I had not heard him do it. As I opened the letters one by one I discovered that there was a draft in one and a bill in another. In fact, I believe each letter had help from the Lord, and the total enabled me to pay all my bills at the end of the month. Praise the Lord for his goodness to the sons of men.

I have already written in an earlier chapter of the remarkable way God supplied a furnished home at the time I was married. The arrangement was that I was to have the furnished home for one year, during which time the owner was on furlough in England. Imagine my surprise then when a cable from England came some time before the year was up indicating that special conditions had caused the missionary to return to Japan earlier than expected, and requesting that I vacate the house right away.

I had made no arrangement for furnishing another home, and had nothing in hand with which to either rent, or to buy the necessary furniture. I was at the crossroads, but praise the Lord, He never fails. After praying about the matter we felt led to take a cottage in the mountains which would postpone the question of renting a house and buying furniture until September. God again proved Himself to be the mighty God. About this time the Japan Rescue Mission started, and Sister Whiteman offered to us rooms rent free in a large house in Karuizawa in return for my help to straighten up their account books.

So here we were again, still without furniture, and without outlay of money, and God had provided a home and our needs.

September 1st this particular year, our eldest daughter, whom we named Faith, was born. A member of the Japan Rescue Mission was a fully qualified English nurse who very kindly and sacrificially attended to my wife at this time. When I informed the nurse that at the moment of Faith's birth we did not have one penny in hand, so that her name

IMPOSSIBILITIES BECOME CHALLENGES

was not only Faith in name, but also in reality, the nurse was so taken aback she did not know what to do.

The summer season at Karuizawa ends with the closing of the month of September. The following months gradually become very cold, and the houses on the whole are not built for cold weather.

It was deemed wise that my wife should not travel for several weeks, which meant that we had to stay in the mountain resort well after the summer season had ended. Finances were tight, but such tight conditions enable us to see the face of Jesus clearer. I well remember when we had come down to nothing, and my wife was still in a very weakened condition. Where to turn was a problem. But God! That very day the missionary across the road came to say good-bye to us, and informed us that he had left in his garden a good deal of cabbages and rhubarb and we were told to help ourselves. Hallelujah, it may seem strange to talk of rhubarb and cabbage for breakfast, and the same for dinner, and then again cabbage and rhubarb for supper, but when God makes the menu, it tastes good. Amen and Amen.

The time came when it was impossible from a physical standpoint to continue in the house we were in. Sister Braithwaite kindly invited us to make her cottage our home for the remainder of the stay in the mountains, God thus again supplying the need.

But a more serious and perhaps the greatest crisis we had yet met in our married life was now facing us. The winter was coming on, and Esther was now able to travel down to the plains. God had made us to know that Yokohama was to be our place of residence as well as of labor for the future. I had not yet attained a working knowledge of Japanese, and it was felt that while for a year we would attend and help in the Sugamo Church, our chief work for the following year was to acquire the language. By renting a house near the beach in Yokohama, we would be assured of quietness and the ability to spend the whole of the day in language study.

MIRACULOUS SUPPLY OF NEEDS

But while these were our convictions we did not have one penny to move from the mountain resort, and even if we had, we did not have a house to go to, and even if we had both the funds for travel, and a house ready for us in Yokohama, we still did not possess the necessary furniture for a home.

We were surely at our wit's end corner. But what a wonderful place that is to be in! And how God loves to surprise His people, and show His mighty power in such times and places.

Much prayer and waiting on God had brought no answer, and I was truly discouraged. I had a newborn baby, a weak wife, and was compelled to leave Karuizawa soon before the snow came, but with neither the means to go, nor a place to call home.

Brother and Sister Adams, holiness missionaries, living in Yokohama, had given us an invitation to stay in their home a few days when we came so that we might look for a house, but added a condition that the devil worked on to make us afraid. The condition was a time limit. They were perfectly willing for us to come until a certain day. But as they were to entertain a number of missionaries passing through on their way to China from a certain date they could not possibly entertain us after that time. That time was drawing dangerously near, and we were still in the mountains without any means.

I received five dollars from America which became 10 Yen in Japanese currency. To exchange this bill I had to spend all the small change I had by buying my railway ticket to the next town where there was a bank that exchanged American bills. My sole possession was now $5.00 (10 Yen). With this in hand I went to the general store in Karuizawa, and purchased a number of articles, including fuel and food. I can see myself now presenting the ten yen bill for the purchase, and the shopkeeper going into an inner room to change the bill, bringing out to me the change in so many silver pieces. There was not the slightest possibility of any mistake, neither the slightest possibility of this shopkeeper knowing my condition. Not a single soul on earth knew my condition, and on the way home I did not meet anyone.

As I entered the house with my purchases I was busy clearing things up and putting the purchases in their places, when over and over again I felt an inward voice telling me to look in my purse. I was busy, trying to get a little supper ready for my wife, and did not at first heed the voice. It was insistent, and became louder. I argued "I know what is in my purse. I bought so many goods, and have so many silver pieces left." And yet the voice was definite, "Look in your purse." Finally, more with the object of silencing the voice than obedience, I did look in my purse, and was surprised to find besides the several silver pieces which represented the change after making my purchases, another 10 Yen bill. I was more than amazed; I was dumbfounded! So much so that I reached for my hat to return to the shopkeeper to give him the bill which I had thought he had not received. But God stopped me, rebuked me for my lack of faith, and made me to know that He had placed the same there.

Right away the conviction as well as the assurance that we should go immediately to Yokohama came to us, using this miraculous 10.00 Yen bill for the transportation charges. When we arrived at Yokohama we just had a few pennies left, and, I believe, just two days before the time limit of the invitation to stay in our friend's home.

The feeling the first morning in this home can never be forgotten. I looked into the newspapers and noticed there was no mail due from abroad for some days. My wife rather smiled at the foolishness of going to look for a house when we did not have one yen in hand to pay down for rent, or "shikikin" (guarantee money). Invariably one had to pay ahead a sum amounting to about three months' rent for guarantee money in renting a house in Japan. This amount is deposited with the landlord who returns it when the house is given up. Occasionally, however, if the landlord feels the tenant to be a fully honest responsible person this guarantee money is waived in lieu of the rent being paid two or three months ahead.

MIRACULOUS SUPPLY OF NEEDS

But I was in no position to do anything, and yet I ventured out that first morning to look for a house, the devil meanwhile whispering in my ear the foolishness of my undertaking. But had not God promised "Lo, I am with you always, even unto the end of the world"? I walked to the beach side of Yokohama, saw a tiny house that was used in winter time for storing fishermen's tackle and nets. In the summer time the house had been rented to Europeans as a bathing pavilion, and contained at least two tiny rooms that would at any rate temporarily serve for a home. I found the landlord, who at first was adverse to renting the place for a home in the winter months. I showed a desire for the same, however, she changed her mind. When I asked her about the renting conditions, I was surprised; I believe I could have been knocked down by a feather, for she said 15.00 Yen monthly, payable at the end of the month, and no guarantee money needed.

I was so happy, I did not know what to do. I just turned right about, and could have run all the way back to our missionary friend's home to tell my wife I had found a home. But on the way God gave the overflow. Hallelujah. While hurrying to where my wife was I was stopped by a European woman, not properly dressed. As this house was near some licensed immoral quarters catering to Europeans, I thought this European lady was accosting me and I turned in the opposite direction. But she persisted and called out, "Are you Mr. Coote?" I could not understand how she knew my name, but finally she told me she had been looking for us for weeks. Brother and Sister Colyer had left Japan, leaving several pieces of furniture for us. Not only had God provided a house, but also furniture, dishes and food, and I had not paid out one single penny. Hallelujah, wonderful Jesus!

We moved to that house, and I believe we had one day to spare on the time limit of our invitation with the missionaries. We had not told them of our circumstances, but God's loving hand had prepared all things for us ahead of time. Praise be unto His holy name.

It was in the same fisherman's cottage that God undertook for us many times. Having a special burden for prayer I left the house one morning with my blanket for the hills. As I left, Esther my wife said, "It is no use coming home for lunch, as I have no money, and nothing whatsoever in the home to get lunch with." I remembered her saying these words, but for some reason they did not enter into my heart, and while I spent the whole of the morning in prayer about some other burdens, I do not remember praying about finances, and came home at noon as usual expecting lunch.

Just as I arrived home, however, I remembered the words spoken by my wife, and rather criticized myself for coming home, as I might have had a longer season of prayer in the hills. However, once home I entered in, and I gazed on several unwrappped parcels. I wondered what they were when I smelt a fine dinner cooking, and thought perhaps my wife was joking after all when she said she had nothing for lunch, for there was certainly a fine dinner on the go.

"Leonard," she called out, "read this note." It was from an ungodly business man working in town. In the note he said how he awoke this particular morning with a very firm conviction he should send out groceries to us, which he did. At ten o'clock the delivery boy came with salt, cheese, and many other things, all just in time because an all seeing eye watches, understands, and makes provisions for every need. Praises!

At the time of the birth of our son David, God again wonderfully proved Himself to be the mighty God of Abraham, Isaac and Jacob. I had in the meantime acquired the language to a certain extent, and God enabled us to rent a little better house in the same district. Our neighbors were American Salvation Army officers. David was born the 14th of December, and finances not being good I decided to take two weeks off the mission work, helping my wife and keeping the home going as best I could.

On Christmas Eve our next door neighbor kindly offered to look after my wife, and the new baby, if I cared to go to the mission for the Christmas exercises. Her

MIRACULOUS SUPPLY OF NEEDS

husband accompanied me, and we came home rather late that night. "Brother Coote," the lady said, "your eldest daughter has a fever, and so I thought it would be wise to keep her in my home tonight." I laid my hands on Faith's head, believed God to undertake, and went home to bed. Early next morning I was hurriedly awakened, and informed that Faith's fever had gone away up, and that she had pneumonia badly. Again I prayed, and the lady was surprised that I did not call for a doctor.

In fact she got vexed that I took the matter so calmly, and then lost her temper, calling me all kinds of names because of what she thought was my indifference to the child's fever. I do not believe it was indifference. This was the first real test along physical lines in the family and I felt like trusting God. However, in a few moments the lady returned bringing her husband with her, who tried to persuade me to place the child in a doctor's care, by insisting that the child had a case of double pneumonia, that his wife was a certified American nurse, who had had much experience with this kind of sickness. They continued by saying that the child would go into convulsions and would die, and terrible slander would be brought on the missionary movement.

These words seemed to be like prophecy. The nurse herself had taken the child's temperature, and was so astonished at the high fever that she dropped the thermometer smashing it, and within a few moments the child went into convulsions!

My wife was still confined to her bed having given birth to our son David two weeks before. "Sister" I said, "whatever is to be done for the child's comfort and welfare, I will do, and follow your directions. Remember the child is in the Lord's hands."

After some time the child quietened down. I then took the opportunity to explain my position to my two Salvation Army officer neighbors. I did so by asking them three questions. They were (1) Have you any money? (2) Are there any mails due from abroad this year? (3) Am I right

IMPOSSIBILITIES BECOME CHALLENGES

in supposing it to be a crime in Japan to leave debts unpaid at the year end?

The reason I asked these questions was to impress the situation I was in upon my neighbors. I said, "I know you have no funds, there is no mail due from abroad this year, and it is considered a crime in Japan to have any debts left over at the year end." The Japanese often travel all night the last day of the year to settle any outstanding debts at that time.

I said, "My position is, I have to pay the rent this month on my home, and on two mission buildings. I have not a penny in hand for this. There is no mail due from abroad the remainder of this year. No one knows my financial condition. I make my needs known only to God, and though the situation seems absolutely impossible in the natural I have one hundred percent faith in God that He will not fail, but by the last day of this year I shall have three rent books fully receipted and my obligations to society met.

"If God has given me faith to do the impossible along financial lines," I continued, "surely this fever that has come on my child is nothing to God. I have preached divine healing, exhorting the saints to trust God for their bodies and for me to fly for medical aid at the first test, surely I would be losing my grip on God, and the saints would lose their faith in me."

So surprised were my neighbors at my financial condition, they nudged each other, as if to say "Let's go home. Coote is in a big mess." And they returned home. A little later, however, the nurse came back, and half apologizing said, "Brother Coote I have had to use drugs two or three times a day all my life for a serious physical condition. I have a very valuable medicine chest filled with drugs and medicines. If your child is alive, well, and running around on New Year's day, I will ask you to pray for me, and you have the privilege of casting my medicine chest into the Pacific Ocean."

We did not see these neighbors again for some days. We knew we were in a battle. We felt that God wanted a

MIRACULOUS SUPPLY OF NEEDS

real testimony to Himself for these dear people who had not known the power of God. The battle was a fierce one and was long and drawn out. We had a new baby just two weeks old, my wife was still in bed recuperating, and Faith was in the grip of a high fever. She would not permit me to come near her bed at night without screaming terribly. We had no help in the house. Cooking, house cleaning, washing, caring for the invalids, all had to be done by myself. Again and again I felt I could not go on, but would go upstairs and fall on my face, and receive new strength from God. Day followed day without funds in hand. I tried my best to pawn my watch, and my wife's wedding ring without avail. However a jeweller did loan us Yen 2.00 on the ring, which enabled me to buy a little food to keep us going during those trying days.

My schedule was to rise early, and pray for God's guidance and help during the day. Then cook a little, wash the baby, and clean up the house, and then walk down town to the post office in the hope that somehow or other a stray letter had come, though there were no mails due from abroad. I did not even have the street car fare, so the journey would take me about an hour there and back. As I did this I would stare into an empty post office box, become a little discouraged, and then turn around, and walk back home. As I entered the home I would hear my wife's weak voice inquiring "Has God honored faith yet?" I would have the utmost difficulty to keep the tears back, for I felt it was hard to bear such a test when in full strength and health, but to do so when one needs special food was even harder. I would then get upstairs as quickly as possible to fall on my knees for more spiritual help from heaven, and go through the routine work for the day.

December 26th, 27th, 28th, alike proved fruitless financially. The devil was ever ready to whisper "Three days more; then two days more, and tomorrow is the last day. What if God doesn't meet the need?" But there is no such phrase "what if" in the realm of faith! Hallelujah! If God has given faith there is no such thing as a possibility of faith failing. Praise the name of the Lord!

IMPOSSIBILITIES BECOME CHALLENGES

I believe it was December 29th. I had gone through the house work routine, and was on my knees before taking the walk down town. "Lord, help me to shout hallelujah as I see an empty post office box today," I prayed, and down town I went. Into the post office I came. I bent low and looked into my box. Empty as it could possibly be! I took off my hat and said "Hallelujah" to the surprise of some people standing near by. Returning home, I was greeted with the same question "Honey, has God undertaken?" and as I nodded my head indicating "not yet," I had the greatest difficulty to show a bold front, to encourage my wife to keep heart in the middle of this test.

Meanwhile Faith's fever had very gradually diminished. I shall never forget what a great encouragement, and an inspiration I received as I noticed an old man, one of the mission saints, silently come day after day, prostrating himself at the rear of Faith's cot, holding on to God for healing and deliverance.

December 30th arrived, and the devil whispered, "Tomorrow is your last day." Again I returned from the post office having seen only an empty post box. The last day of the year arrived. It was with a trembling heart I left the house after praying again, telling God that I did believe Him.

As I arrived at the post office I hesitated a moment outside, and prayed for strength. This was the last day, and as usual I saw simply an empty post box. For a few moments my faith flew away, my hands fell helpless at my side, and I did not know what to do. I thought I could bear the failure alone, but what would I say to my wife who was not strong?

I hesitated at the post office, wondering what to do, when one of the swinging doors caught my foot. Then I heard my named called, "Is that you, Mr. Coote?" I gladly answered and found that a money order for $30.00 had just come through and though it was payable through another post office, I urged the clerk to get it through for me right away, and how the joy bells began ringing in my soul!

MIRACULOUS SUPPLY OF NEEDS

On my way home I paid my rent and bought some tea and biscuits. As I arrived home I invited my next door neighbor to come at once. She acted a little surprised at the urgent invitation. I got Faith dressed up in her best, and when my guest arrived, she was stunned to see Faith up playing. She said, "Is this Faith?" "Yes," I answered. "She is still a little weak, but God has wonderfully undertaken for her. Besides this, see these rent books, they are all fully paid."

"Well, Brother Coote," she said, "that is fine but Faith's sickness could not have been pneumonia, for it could not have been healed in so short a time," and so again unbelief tried to do away with the power of God, and the vow to get rid of the medicine chest was never fulfilled.

CHAPTER TWELVE

STUDYING THE LANGUAGE

*"Study to shew thyself approved unto God, a
workman that needeth not to be ashamed,
rightly dividing the word of truth."*
(2 Timothy 2:15)

God had distinctly led me to give one whole year to the
study of the Japanese language. After leaving business the
mind of the Lord for me then was that I should not open my
own work or study the language, but give my whole time to
prayer, and the study of the Word until Japan received an
outpouring of the Holy Ghost.

God had now graciously met scores of Japanese, (it
could be easily said hundreds) filling them with the Holy
Ghost as on the day of Pentecost. This work had been
accomplished by my using an interpreter, but now the time
had come for me to preach and teach directly in the
Japanese language, for there were various problems arising
that could only be faced as they were dealt with in the native
tongue.

Further it was laid heavily on my heart that the call of
God was not merely that I should become a missionary to
the Japanese people, but as the call itself indicated "Japan
and Pentecost until Jesus comes," to the whole of the
Japanese empire. Hitherto God had enabled me to witness
to the Pentecostal power in the various towns situated in
various sections of the country, but Japan as a nation had
not yet been touched. It was very clear that a mission here
and there and a handfull of foreign missionaries was far
from fulfilling the Great Commission outlined in the
twenty-eighth chapter of Matthew.

Besides the great burden of Japanese being filled with
the Holy Ghost, there arose the further burden of pioneering into untouched territories with the full gospel, and of
establishing missions and churches standing for the full

STUDYING THE LANGUAGE

truth. In order to do this it was evident that I had to get the language.

Though I had been in Japan six years I was yet unable to speak Japanese. I had made many attempts while in business to study the language, and also as a missionary. But for some reason or other, I never made any headway, usually became discouraged, and gave up.

But now the conviction grew that it was a question of life or death. And the Lord permitted me to take one year off from active evangelistic work, to devote myself entirely to the study of the language. I was unable financially to hire expensive teachers, or even to go to special schools that are arranged for foreign missionaries. However I found someone willing to give me one hour two days a week and setting my mind to the matter, gave the whole of the day to intensive study. I refused to see anybody in the daytime, refused to be interrupted by anything or anybody, and my own wife had to be willing to only speak to me at meal times or make the afternoon walk a language test.

By this means I managed to break the back of what is considered one of the most difficult languages in the world. No one can imagine, however, what struggles, heartaches, and battles I went through during this year. I would pray through every morning, then make the upstairs of my home my study. Here I would learn by heart some phrase from the Japanese school primer, and pace up and down the room until I could say it from memory without hesitation. The next day I would review what I had learned by heart the previous day, and invariably I would not be able to remember more than a couple of words.

I was constantly discouraged, but as constantly the Spirit of God would grant me a stronger determination to master my difficulties, and praise the Lord at the close of the year I found myself in a position where I had to use the language I had acquired.

I felt led at the close of the year to pitch a tent in the city of Yokohama. My worker and former interpreter was to come from Tokyo nightly to help in the campaign. But

IMPOSSIBILITIES BECOME CHALLENGES

his wife came down with a deathly sickness right at the beginning of the meetings, so that he was unable to come every night as arranged. This left me with the tent filled with people, and with a broken knowledge of the language, but praise the Lord, I also had a passion for souls.

I accepted the challenge as from God, and preached the best I could. I was told by one or two that they could only catch a word here and there, which they figured out was Japanese, but honestly for them to say that they knew what I was talking about, they could not. To be told this not once, but often, would be enough to destroy the faintest speck of enthusiasm there might be left in me. I would pour into my heart the fire of God. I determined even though I could not make them understand with my voice, I would show such enthusiasm, and real earnestness that they would thus take notice, and come under the power of God.

Whether the people understood or not, the power of God did came down, twelve were baptized in water and ten of them received the baptism of the Holy Ghost. It was a wonderful meeting! I do not believe I shall ever forget it, especially as it was the first tent meeting in which I attempted to preach Christ directly in the Japanese language!

The neighbors found out that we went to prayer at a certain time every night, and that God's power was manifested. They would then gather in hundreds to watch the manifestations of God. They would not come early enough to listen to the preaching, but would time their arrival when the seekers were on their faces, crying and repenting of their sins, and others coming under the power of God.

The crowds became so great at this time, that the police interfered, and finally stopped the tent meetings, insisting that the crowd that gathered at the time of prayer was too great for public safety. The tent meeting stopped, but the power kept coming. We transferred the meetings to our home, and the seekers came, and many were blessed and filled with the Spirit.

STUDYING THE LANGUAGE

Of all the miracles that the Lord has performed in my life and ministry, this one concerning the language I truly believe can be reckoned as one of the greatest. I cannot exaggerate how impossible it seemed to acquire the Japanese language. Even studying as I was ten and twelve hours a day and longer, it seemed absolutely foolish to go on. Friends have told me in recent days, that is, those who knew me in the early days, that they are absolutely amazed for they were very sure that I would never be able to speak in Japanese.

CHAPTER THIRTEEN

THE YOKOHAMA REVIVAL

*"I will pour water upon him that is thirsty, and
floods upon the dry ground: I will pour
my Spirit upon thy seed, and my
blessing upon thine offspring."*
(Isaiah 44:3)

The tent meeting in which I first preached Christ in the Japanese language really became the beginning of a revival in the city of Yokohama, which kept on until the great earthquake which destroyed the city.

God honored our efforts and a dozen people were baptized in water. Our next step was to open a mission which became the center of the revival.

It is interesting to recall how God provided a helper for us in this work. My former interpreter was now the pastor of the Sugamo Church and I was paying special attention to the Yokohama work. A knock came at the door of my home early one morning and a young man asked me if it was a church. When I answered in the negative he apologized saying when he heard someone praying he thought it must be a place of worship. He was a business man that was facing tremendous issues, and was at the point of suicide. My praying arrested him, and repenting of his sins, he was baptized in the Spirit, and led to help me in the Yokohama work.

A young fellow who had infrequently attended other churches, but had not received full satisfaction in his soul came to the tent one night. He heard of the baptism of the Spirit. He came again. The second night, he received the baptism of the Spirit, and spoke with other tongues. The following morning the Spirit of God awoke him very early, bidding him go and tell his experiences to some of his acquaintances. This he did, and they were amazed, and immediately began to look into the matter.

THE YOKOHAMA REVIVAL   97

About 8:30 a.m., just as we had finished breakfast, this young fellow came with five others, telling me they had come to learn about the Holy Ghost. The Spirit witnessed that God had sent them, and I said, "Let us go to the hills, and see what the Word says about it." I took my blanket and my Bible, and when I found out they had come from the holiness church I emphasized the question of the baptism of the Spirit as revealed in the book of the Acts of the Apostles.

Half an hour of teaching led one or two of them to ask for prayer, and right then and there on the mountain side, though these brethren had never attended a Pentecostal meeting, they came under the power of God, and all, with one exception were baptized with the Spirit, and spoke with other tongues.

We had now quite a nucleus for the new mission, and the revival went on in the mission. Two daughters of a wealthy contractor found the Lord. He himself was a terrible drinker, and was hardly ever sober.

This fact, undoubtedly, led the daughters to seek hope in Christ. They were 19 and 21 years of age respectively.

The father grew enraged at their accepting Christ. One night he forced a crisis. At midnight he called the girls to him. "Tonight, you decide between Christ and your physical father. Decide for Christ, and you leave this home without a penny or even any clothes. Decide for me, and all is yours." The girls pleaded with him as they urged him to reconsider his decision. The girls testified to the joy and peace that they had found in Christ, and for this reason they could not give up their faith.

But the father was adamant. That night the girls were cast out of their home for the name of Jesus. The father then attributed the girls' faith and refusal to obey him to the mission, and to myself as the missionary. His opposition grew in intensity. He hired wicked men to create a disturbance around the mission in order to have the mission closed, and threatened to murder all who would dare to side with us.

IMPOSSIBILITIES BECOME CHALLENGES

For a time a reign of terror surrounded the mission, and the weaker believers were keenly tested, the numbers decreasing. But the faithful ones kept on, the workers gave themselves to prayer, and the devil had to find other ways of destroying what God had started.

As I visited the mission one morning for Bible study with the workers, I noticed everybody was silent. Besides, windows were broken, hymn books and Bibles were torn, and the whole place resembled more a battle field than a mission hall. We could not help but wonder what had taken place. Then we found some of the workers in bed, tired, and bruised. The bullies hired by the drunkard father, had broken into the mission about two in the morning, and had given the workers a good beating in their efforts to destroy the mission.

We were now in a hand battle with the enemy. These bullies became braver in their efforts, waiting for the right moment in the meeting to yell at the top of their voices to try to frighten the worshippers. One Sunday evening while the message was being given I noticed a wriggling snake beneath the benches. This would have sent everybody scattering in all directions, but by God's grace I was able to keep quiet, and with the help of one Christian got the serpent out of the building without anyone else knowing what had happened.

On another Sunday evening, sensing that trouble was brewing I asked my worker to preach, while I acted as doorkeeper. Soon the bullies arrived, and did their best to destroy the meeting. I managed by guile to lead them away from the meeting place, and suddenly when quite a distance away from the mission one of the bullies gave me a distinct knock-out blow across my right cheek. Remembering the words of scripture, I thanked him for the blow, and begged him for another on the other side of my face, praying for strength and grace to receive it. It never came, but instead I received a running kick in the stomach.

We praised the Lord for these persecutions, as we were conscious they were signs of revival. And the revival came,

THE YOKOHAMA REVIVAL

and carried us through to the earthquake itself. Another tent campaign was held, and souls were mightily convicted, wonderfully saved, and filled with the Holy Ghost. All praises be unto Jesus. Out of this second tent campaign two young men who were ignorant of the gospel were wonderfully brought in, baptized, filled with the Holy Ghost, and today they occupy positions of pastors in their own independent churches in the cities of Kyoto and Osaka.

We advertised this second tent campaign as "Everlasting Life Meeting." A would be suicide was on his way to destroy his life the very day of the opening of the meeting. His attention was arrested, he attended the meetings and found a full and free salvation.

God gave me particular authority in this second Yokohama Tent Campaign to preach repentance, water baptism in the name of the Lord Jesus Christ, and the gift of the baptism of the Holy Ghost. As I preached Christ and His Cross night after night, I would invite those who repented of their sins to come forward, deal with God at the altar, and prepare for water baptism. I repeatedly told them not to come forward if they had not fully repented of their sins. I exhorted them to rather come to the meeting another night than to come forward, and try to pray conviction off their souls.

A well built, fine looking lumber man came to me at the altar. "Cannot I pray, Mr. Coote?" he asked. "Well, did you repent?" I enquired. "No, not yet," he answered, "but I want to pray." "No," I said, "you come again tomorrow night, and then perhaps you will be able to repent."

He came again the second night, and made the same request. He said, "As I hear you preach I feel worse. I do so badly want to pray." But I said, "Did you repent?" "No," he replied, "I cannot repent yet." "Then, go home, and come again, tomorrow night," I told him.

The third night he did not appear, and the devil teased me that I had been a little too radical with him. However I left the matter with the Lord, and went on helping with the

IMPOSSIBILITIES BECOME CHALLENGES

souls at the altar, when to my astonishment I saw this fine well-built lumber man at the end of the line, crying as if his heart would break. "I do repent," he was crying out to God. "That is fine," I thought, and praised God, and just left him with the Lord.

When men repent they go right on with God. They will not quibble about being baptized. They will not wonder whether one tenth is too much to give to God. Repentance is the best beginning for obedience. It was then quite natural that on the following morning, this man should present himself at our home, saying, "Now Mr. Coote, I am ready for water baptism." Hallelujah! God was true to His Word! When this young fellow took God at His Word, was baptized in the name of Jesus for the remission of sins, (read Acts 2:38), the Holy Ghost came down upon him in the water, and he too spoke with other tongues and glorified God.

The drunken father found out that his method of persecution was helping us in our work, instead of destroying it, so he changed his tactics. He hired a newspaper to give us a dirty write-up, and laid a trap for me. I was caught in the trap, but God made the snare to turn out for His glory and praise.

One afternoon two representatives of one of the largest newspapers visited me at my home. They told me that their newspaper had decided to run a religious column in their paper once a week, and each church in the city would be given an opportunity to describe themselves, and state the reason for their existence. They said they had decided to give me the following Thursday's column, and asked me for particulars of the work, as well as a photograph of myself and my wife. These were gladly given, as we were unaware that the whole thing was a snare of the enemy.

The next morning one of our workers showed to us a copy of the morning paper, issued by one of the newspapers with a circulation of one million. The article written against us and the Pentecostal Church was on an important page, covering all five columns, and going down to almost one

THE YOKOHAMA REVIVAL 101

fourth of the page. It contained my photograph and supposedly my personal testimony accepting the accusations against us. We were supposed to have peculiar power over women, a sort of mesmerism. Once women came under such a power they did exactly as we told them.

This paper article was copied by smaller newspapers, I saw it in as many as 30 different newspapers.

My wife also was supposed to have given the newspaper her testimony saying that she became my wife by this method of mesmerism. Anyway, the article was of sufficient interest that it was copied by as many as a dozen other newspapers in the night issue.

As the article contained my photograph I was in the eyes of the public for some time. On the street, or on tram cars people would nudge each other, and say "There is that man." But praise the Lord, the devil oversteps himself, and two school teachers, both ladies, who saw the article, were so interested, as they knew this could not possibly be true, came to the mission. They repented of their sins, were baptized in water, and baptized in the Holy Ghost, speaking with other tongues as the Spirit gave utterance. The newspaper article therefore did not harm us one bit, but rather helped to advertise the work. How true is God's Word,

"For we can do nothing against the truth, but for the truth" (2 Corinthians 13:8).

Baptismal services were now being held every day, and sometimes as often as twice and three times a day. My baptismal clothes hardly had time to dry. God was surely giving Yokohama a wonderful opportunity of salvation before He shook every building in the city. Remember, this revival was being carried on right up to the day of the earthquake in which Yokohama and part of Tokyo were destroyed.

Conviction for a further tent campaign was received, ground sought, and funds prayed for that it might be held. But finances did not permit the campaign to be held. Friends hearing of our desire to keep on evangelizing right

102   IMPOSSIBILITIES BECOME CHALLENGES

through Japan's dreadful summer wrote to me letters of
exhortation: "You ought to have a rest. Why not visit with
your family in the mountains for a month or so? Take
things easy." These exhortations were appreciated. I was
really tired in body, and my nerves would not be the worse
for a good rest. But the firm conviction that I should go
through the great heat, and evangelize, even if not in a tent
meeting, at best in the mission hall, was still with me, and I
must obey the Lord.

Since my final efforts for getting ground for tent meetings failed, special efforts were made in the mission. All the
saints were alive to the situation. Many came early nightly
for special prayer. I formed as many as four open air bands
every night, and the leader of each band had a watch. I
arranged for the leader of the open air band to stop his
street meeting at a certain time, bring his crowd down a
certain street, where he would be met by street band No. 2.
Joining together they would go on down the street until
they met street band No. 3 who in turn would join with the
crowd, and before arriving at the hall they would meet
street band No. 4.

This arrangement was carried on night after night for a
week in Yokohama, just a week or so before the great
earthquake. We crowded the street with people so that the
automobiles hardly had room to move. The mission was
jammed to capacity night after night, and God worked.
One night I shall never forget. One of my workers
preached. He simply told his testimony, and just before he
closed a well-dressed man rushed forward to the altar and
cried out to God "Oh God, please forgive me; I am a
murderer of 800 people." We were all astonished, and
could not make out what he meant. How could one man
murder 800 others without being caught by the police, and
still not be in prison, or the gallows? We found out
afterwards that he was a headmaster in a primary school,
and had been a very enthusiastic teacher of idols to the
children, taking them to the temples, and exhorting them to
bow down to idols. That night he saw his mistake, realized
that there was a living God, and in his terrible conviction

THE YOKOHAMA REVIVAL   103

felt his responsibility for the 800 children under his care.
The second night he came to the meeting, he received the
baptism of the Holy Ghost.

Persecution broke out from another angle. We were
baptizing in the sea in the heat of the summer. The power
would come down on the seekers and they would come up
out of the water speaking with other tongues. One day
some German business men took exception to our meetings, and praises, and called a European doctor. He made a
demonstration before the crowd; supposedly took the
pulses of the seekers and threatened to have me put in jail
for baptizing Japanese in the cold sea water. His standpoint
was utterly ridiculous for not many yards away from us were
hundreds of bathers who had been in the water for hours.
True, our converts were shaking, but they were not shaking
because of the cold, but because of the heat, the fire of God
being on their bodies.

Some letters were sent to the English press about this
and some days later detectives came to our house, and we
learned that efforts had been made to have me deported
from Japan as undesirable. But we knew of higher
authorities, who were working on our behalf, who had
promised "Lo I am with you always, even unto the end of
the world." Amen and amen.

It was now the general understanding among the
Christians that when a man truly repented of his sins, was
baptized in the all powerful name of Jesus for the remission
of his sins, he would be baptized with the Holy Ghost. Just
before retiring one night a man came to see me. We still
lived on the beach, in a rather lonely place, and I could not
understand who this visitor would be. "Who is it?" I called
out. "Hallelujah," was the reply. That settled the question.
One of the Christians had brought a young fellow to be
baptized. That is scriptural, is it not, to be baptized at
midnight? (Read Acts 16:33).

I had an hour's talk with the young man, and soon found
out that he was ready for baptism, repenting fully of his sins.
The night is one to be remembered. It was pitch black, not

IMPOSSIBILITIES BECOME CHALLENGES

a star in the sky. I remember how I had to almost crawl on my hands and knees to find the water, and could not see my candidate as I baptized; it was truly a night of oriental darkness. As we two stood in the water, I said, "Brother, here is the Word of the Lord."

"Now when they heard this, they were pricked in their heart, and said unto Peter and to the rest of the apostles, men and brethren, what shall we do? Then Peter said unto them: Repent, and be baptized every one of you in the name of Jesus Christ for the remission of sins, and ye shall receive the gift of the Holy Ghost" (Acts 2:37,38).

"Have you repented?" I asked my candidate. "Do you believe that God will honor the name of Jesus, recognize your heart of repentance, and grant to you the gift of the Holy Ghost?" His answer being in the affirmative, I baptized him in the name of Jesus Christ for the remission of sins. I heard the water splash, and the next noise I heard was this brother speaking with other tongues and glorifying God. Hallelujah.

I remember another case, that of a young fellow who wished to be baptized, and together we went to the beach. I was not altogether satisfied with his repentance, although he gave me the assurance that everything was all right.

As we came up from the water there was no evidence of power, and my doubts were increased. "Brother," I said, "you tell me that you have repented, and yet you do not receive any power from heaven. God's Word tells me that if we repent, and are baptized in Jesus' Name for the remission of sins, we shall receive the gift of the Holy Ghost. Something must be wrong. Either God is a liar, or you are. Which is it?" "I am positive I have repented," he insisted. "Well then, what shall we say? If you insist that you have repented, and God has not given you the Holy Ghost, and there is no evidence of power, or of the presence of the Spirit, and I, too, have no witness of the presence of the Spirit, shall we say God has not honored His Word?" The young man saw my point, and breaking down, exclaimed, "True, I am the liar, I have not fully

THE YOKOHAMA REVIVAL

repented, and have some confessions to make." He told me what they were, and he dealt with God right then and there, and immediately the power came, and he was baptized in the Holy Ghost, speaking with other tongues.

READY FOR STREET MEETING

CHAPTER FOURTEEN

THE GREAT JAPANESE EARTHQUAKE

*"And after the earthquake a fire; but the Lord
was not in the fire; and after the
fire a still small voice."
(I Kings 19:12)*

Japan is a land of earthquakes. And it is not an uncommon thing to feel one's house shaking, or to be walking down a street and notice houses jumping up and down. The resident of any length in Japan will doubtless experience awaking in the middle of the night to find everything around him shaking like a leaf. But the earthquake of 1923 was something greater. The official figures of those known to be killed reached above 100,000 people not including Europeans and Chinese.

The city of Yokohama was entirely destroyed. Two thirds of Tokyo was destroyed and hundreds of villages and towns within 70 or 80 miles were devastated. When I have spoken of this earthquake in America and England, some have thought that the extent of the earthquake had been exaggerated by the news reports, but the extent of the damage was so great, this was impossible.

The object of this chapter is to recount my personal experience in the earthquake and to magnify the power of God. The same God Who supplied our needs in times of safety also supplied in the time of destruction, confusion and disaster. Praise His holy name.

God had led us to have a special evangelistic campaign in the middle of August when the heat was almost unbearable. The messages peculiarly all bore on the circumstances surrounding the Second Coming of Christ, and the Tribulation coming upon the world. One night I emphasized how men would seek death and not be able to die, and would even gnaw their tongues with anger at the living God.

THE GREAT JAPANESE EARTHQUAKE 107

Little did I know that in a few days, these prophecies from the book of Revelation would have a local fulfillment. Surely it was the Spirit of God urging us to exhort the sinners to flee from the wrath to come, and to believe in Jesus, the only Savior.

The first day of September opened as any ordinary day. It was a Saturday, and as the great heat of August had begun to wane a little, businessmen were hurriedly placing their books and accounts into their safes ready to leave the office at prompt noon for an afternoon's recreation. At the same time wives were busily engaged over kitchen fires preparing their husbands' lunches. Thousands of Japanese workmen whose work did not stop at noon on Saturday as do the foreign businesses, little thought that a disaster of the greatest magnitude was upon them.

At 11:59 the earth gave one great reel, and the whole city of Yokohama fell flat on the ground like a pack of cards blown by the wind. Only three buildings in the whole city remained in tact. The mighty God had moved His little finger and a city of thousands of inhabitants lay in ruins. And not only the city of Yokohama, but hundreds of towns and villages in the area, including half of the immense city of Tokyo were laid flat.

It is almost impossible to imagine what took place in the following hours. Whole families found themselves pinned under piles of debris, containing heavy tiles, large wooden timbers, one or two of the members killed outright, while others lay with limbs smashed. The head of the house himself after wriggling from under this mass of debris would stand beside what was once his home, and possibly his workshop as well, dazed. What had happened? Where was he? As the truth in all its grim reality dawned upon him, possibly by hearing the moans of his dying wife pinned under some exceeding heavy lumber, he would work with what strength he had left to release her from this condition. A mass of earth (as Japanese walls are made of mud), had to be removed, then timbers, and tiles. He would be further shocked by what he saw not many yards away: the right hand of his eighteen year old daughter. The hand had

IMPOSSIBILITIES BECOME CHALLENGES

been clean cut off by falling timbers when the house fell. Undaunted, he worked on, finally reaching the body of his wife. Limbs were broken, and she was dying, moaning her last moans. The earthquake affected all alike, hospitals, fire stations, ambulances, all were thrown into the greatest confusion, so that there was no help for anyone. The hopelessness of the situation met by the Japanese at this time - (thousands of whom had never heard of the comfort of Jesus) - can never be estimated.

Families were entirely separated. Husbands were unable to locate what once was their homes. Remaining families had to flee from the oncoming fire, and seek shelter where they could. It was a tremendously pitiable sight, days and weeks after the earthquake to witness men, women and children of all ages walking up and down amidst the ruins of Yokohama with billboards advertising the fact they had lost their mother or husband or some children, wandering hither and thither, oftentimes in vain hopes that their loved ones had found refuge from the terrible flames that devoured more people than the earthquake.

And even now, many years later the newspapers still tell of reconciliations among family members who have been separated all these years, thinking the other party was dead.

Just prior to the earthquake I had been able to get away to the hills for a few days of quiet and rest. The night before the quake found us with but a few pennies in hand. One of my workers had gotten my mail and forwarded it to the hills where we were staying, but I never received it as it was burnt along with the post office and other buildings.

We were in a couple of rooms sharing a small cottage with another missionary in Karuizawa. Just as we were eating lunch the house began to sway and I got the family out to the neighbor's lawn next door. We were 80 miles from the center of the quake, yet quite a few small Japanese houses were demolished. I had a peculiar feeling about the quake but said nothing. At dusk I took a walk and saw a strange sight away across the fields. What I saw

THE GREAT JAPANESE EARTHQUAKE 109

must have been 80 miles away. It appeared like a huge mountain on fire. Later we found out that it was Tokyo in a blaze of fire.

Tokyo and Yokohama being so thickly populated, the fires that followed the quake enveloped the cities. Refugees told stirring stories of the procession of people fleeing the oncoming flames. Mothers with young infants were in the crowd, pressed on by the procession from behind. Tired and faint they became weary and in some cases the babies held in their arms fell on the ground only to be trampled to death by the oncoming multitude.

One of the most unsightly things I saw upon my arrival in Yokohama was the scorched bodies of men and women who burned to death.

After thirty days after the earthquake I still counted four or five large fires burning stacks of coal, and I even stumbled over the burned body of a European woman.

The second day of September the news spread throughout Karuizawa: "Yokohama wiped out by earthquake." Who can tell my feelings? I had just been through some of the worst persecution I had ever witnessed, though praise God, I had also seen some of the mightiest works of God in that city. Now the news had come that the whole city was wiped out. My first thought was that I should immediately go down to the city and see what had become of our converts. This seemed ridiculous from the natural. I had not more than a couple of yen in hand, and there was no possibility now of receiving incoming mails, for the whole postal system in the Yokohama area was completely disorganized. But nothing on earth, in the sky or sea can stop the upward look of faith in God.

When the shock of the first news of the destruction hit us, my wife and I knelt down in the small room where we were staying and prayed: "Lord, show us the next city where you want us to go."

I felt I ought to go that very night to Yokohama. But I needed at least Yen 6.00 for a return ticket. A missionary lady who did not know our financial situation gave me Yen

110   IMPOSSIBILITIES BECOME CHALLENGES

10.00 that very day, which provided not only the fare down, but a little extra to have some chocolates in my pocket for sustenance as I did not know how I would eat when I arrived.

The train started at midnight, and ordinarily should have arrived four hours later. However we did not arrive at two or three stations this side of Tokyo until seven in the morning, and I had been standing up with hardly an inch of breathing space all night. Hundreds of people were flocking to Tokyo to see what they could do for relatives and friends. In the crush of the train I lost my hat. Rumors were out that Koreans had taken this opportunity to regain their independence from Japan and were pouring poison into the wells and setting fire to remaining buildings.

We were not able to travel further than 10 miles this side of Tokyo. We left the train tired and hungry. I realized that I would soon be laid low by the heat of the sun if I did not get a hat. But that seemed well nigh an impossibility. All around me were tumbled down houses and hardly a house without extensive damage. Finally I saw a small shop that sold baby clothes, and managed to get a baby hat that at least protected my head from the terrible sun and I started on my long walk of 30 miles to Yokohama.

Nothing special happened the first day. Devastation was to be seen everywhere. I had prepared by carrying a bottle of water on my back, and this with the chocolates in my pocket helped me to keep up my strength. Dusk came along and I was still a long way from my destination.

As dusk came I noticed that young men had formed themselves into a volunteer army or police force, forming barricades, and all travelers were strictly questioned as to their motives for going forward. Occasionally as I was questioned at these barricades I was asked to drink the water from my bottle to prove it was not poison. At first I thought it to be a huge joke, but as the quizzing became stricter with the coming of darkness, I realized that my future pathway was not going to be easy.

THE GREAT JAPANESE EARTHQUAKE

Finally I came to a standstill. One of the chief men at a certain barricade refused to accept my story or permit me to go forward. To return was impossible, and I wondered what to do. I had in my pocket a letter addressed to the British Consul in Yokohama, from the missionaries gathered in Karuizawa. I appealed to the volunteer young men with this letter, and they allowed me to go forward. I was now very tired, and realized I was still a long way from my destination. I also realized it was dangerous to attempt to force my way through that night.

Those volunteer police all had some kind of weapons. At first they were only sticks, but as I drew nearer the city of Yokohama, and it became darker these volunteer police carried drawn swords. The nearer I got to Yokohama, the more dangerous was the traveling. The barricades became tighter and tighter and appeared every few yards.

Rumors were flying that the Koreans, whom the Japanese hated, were poisoning all the wells as a retaliation for what the Japanese military had done to their country. That was the reason that I was commanded to drink the water out of my bottle every time I passed a barricade. Finally, I realized that I had come as far as I dared to go. At the last barricade, while surly volunteer military men questioned my purpose for going to Yokohama, and accusing me of being in league with the Koreans in their poisoning operations, they pushed an open sword right to my heart. Just one more short push and I realized that my life would be ended.

Fortunately another Japanese who evidently knew the neighborhood went through the barricade at the same time and he strongly advised me not to attempt to go any further, for, he declared, I, being a European, and the Japanese being excited about what the Koreans were supposedly doing, he felt sure that I would not arrive at my destination alive. He kindly offered to give me shelter for the night in the neighborhood and I considered it was wise to accept his kindness and followed him away from·the main road into a village.

IMPOSSIBILITIES BECOME CHALLENGES

But what a night I had. I can sincerely say that it was the worst night that I have ever had in my whole life. After arriving at what seemed to be an acquaintance of his he refreshed himself by washing his hands and face in the yard. There were absolutely no lights, and I realized I was in a strange place amid strange people with just the light of one thin candle. This friend took his time in washing himself and spent at least an hour describing how he had met many of the Koreans and how he had killed them. If this description had just been a matter of destroying their lives it would have been bad indeed, but it was more than that. He told how he had met Koreans and had demanded at the point of the sword for them to strip themselves of their clothes. He then told how he took his sword and cut their bodies in two, starting from the middle of the head. He revelled in his description of the disembowelment of his victims. He glowed over the fact of the large number that he had thus dealt with, and then he showed me inside to a narrow pallet, just large enough for one person to sleep on. Under this pallet he laid his bloody sword, and laid down beside me - he to sleep, but I desperately tired out, trying hard to keep one eye open during the night.

I realized that if the story I had heard him relate was at all true, and his sword seemed to indicate that it was, he would have some horrible dreams in the middle of the night, awake in one of those dreams and think that perhaps I was another Korean. How wonderful it is to be able to commit oneself into the hands of an Almighty God, knowing that He never slumbers nor sleeps. Praise His holy name. However, I must have fallen asleep in the early hours of the morning for I awakened with a start with shouts of men's voices in the neighborhood. I listened and the voices drew nearer and nearer. At last I was able to distinguish what was being said. "The Koreans are coming; out everybody and let us butcher them." I kept as still as I possibly could and pled the blood. My friend lying at my side was still sleeping, but not for long. Soon he stirred as the voices repeated the aforementioned statement. I wondered if the beating of my heart had awakened him.

THE GREAT JAPANESE EARTHQUAKE   113

Without a word he jumped up, grabbed his sword and out of the house he went, evidently on another murderous expedition. I could not feel it was safe to stay where I was. I felt that I had better get out of the house for it must soon be morning. I did this very gingerly not knowing the geography of the house. It was still dark, but soon I was out on the open road again.

The little rest I had received during the night enabled me to walk the remaining distance fairly easily, although there was no possibility of eating or drinking. Everywhere I saw the remains of the terrible earthquake. Not a house standing; nothing but rubble was to be seen all along the journey. It was with difficulty, after reaching the city of Yokohama, that I found where my mission had been. I finally did reach the place only to find nothing left but cinders. All mission property, the tent, personal belongings, everything had all gone up in smoke. But what a privilege to stand on that same site, and realize that God's grace had been sufficient to preach the Gospel in the extreme heat to those who would face horrible death in the earthquake. How I thanked God for the privilege of warning the heathen to flee from the wrath to come through the redemptive work of Calvary.

While I stood there praying a man came up to me. "Do you recognize me?" were his first words. For a moment I did not. Then he explained that he was one of the young men who had endeavored to hinder the meetings the immediate period before the earthquake. He confessed that he felt that I was crazy talking about the conditions that were prophesied to take place before the end of the world. He then added, "But now I know you were telling the truth, for I have experienced exactly what you said."

Wending my way from where my mission had stood to where my home was situated was a job indeed. Everything was rubble. Dead bodies could be seen everywhere. As I passed by a park I was particularly impressed with the large number of bodies burnt and lying around. I knew the park well as it faced the Y.M.C.A. where I often ate lunch. There were no buildings, save a small hut in the park, and I began to wonder how so many people could have been burnt there. Either the flames were so great that they jumped over the park, or the flames came out of the earth. There was practically nothing in the park itself that would carry the flames. The fact of what took place, proven by the scores of bodies lying around, brought a great awe to my own heart, especially as God had so marvellously blessed in the special meetings that had been held right up to the time of the earthquake. Surely it was God who had caused me to preach to the people night after night about the terrible oncoming judgments of God, and the period of tribulation still to come to this earth.

I continued on the way to my home but found out that the burnable parts of the bridge over which I had to cross to get to my home were gone and the only way now was to crawl on my hands and knees across iron girders. It was a risky business for as I looked down into the waters they were filled with hundreds of corpses and one misstep would have meant that I would fall in the midst of them. God gave grace to get across the bridge and find my home. It was still standing though partially wrecked. The fires had not come to where we lived. In a few days practically all the Christians had registered at this home, some seventy or eighty of them. We investigated very closely, but as far as we could tell not one man or woman or child among our converts, who had been baptized in the name of Jesus Christ, and who had been baptized in the Holy Ghost, had lost their lives.

When it is realized that today the official number of those known to be dead is as high as 100,000 people, and as our Christians resided in various parts of Yokohama, it is a glorious testimony to the power of God and to the reality of the baptism of the Holy Ghost, as well as to the name of Jesus, when we were able to register all the Christians and were unable to find any who had lost their lives in this great earthquake. All glory be unto God. But may this fact be impressed upon our hearts more and more, for a greater earthquake is due this old earth, and tribulations of a worse nature are in God's program for the future.

THE GREAT JAPANESE EARTHQUAKE　　115

It is so easy in times of safety to speak disparagingly of the sign of speaking in other tongues, or the wonderful name of Jesus, but when disaster arrives, and death is seen on every hand, for a band of seventy to eighty Christians of all ages and from all walks of life, to come through untouched, unharmed, rejoicing in God, and praising the Lord, this, I believe, is a glorious testimony to the reality and truth of these points of doctrine.

Surely it is as the Word of God states,

"The name of the Lord is a strong tower: the righteous runneth into it, and is safe" (Proverbs 18:10).

God literally performed miracles in this earthquake to supply our needs. The recording of them brings anew a joy to my heart and fresh praises to my lips. As I have mentioned, prior to the earthquake we had gone through keen financial tests. These had left us practically penniless at the time of the quake itself. However, just two or three weeks before the quake, I noticed a sale of groceries from America, which had been damaged by sea water and the prices were ridiculously cheap.

I was unable to buy much as my finances did not permit this, but I was able to purchase a little. Twenty or thirty refugees sought safety in our home, and the provisions that I had bought cheaply at the sale were already there waiting to feed this band of Christians. Hallelujah. Praise the Lord. Had they not been there, the Christians would have had to do without food.

Our landlord at that time was a very old resident of Yokohama, a Britisher, who had made a success in business and was practically retired. Whenever we paid the monthly rent he was always willing for a chat, and if in winter time would invite us to sit around the fire as he had an English fireplace in his home. He asked us many questions about ourselves, our work, and our method of support, and would invariably smile at our "living by faith," and praying in money. As we were renting his house he did not openly oppose us, but we knew inwardly he thought we were very strange people.

116 IMPOSSIBILITIES BECOME CHALLENGES

After I had been back in the earthquake area a couple of days it came to me to go and visit him and see how he was getting along. I found that his eldest son had been knocked down by the quake and killed, and that he and his wife were in the tumbled down house, suffering from lack of food. The bank had thousands upon thousands of his money, but money in those days was absolutely of no use. I shall never forget how dignified I felt as I ran home and carried to my wealthy landlord a five pound tin of corn meal and some other tinned supplies that my "living by faith" had made provision for, whereas all his money was lying in the bank and could not buy a morsel of bread.

When I arrived at what was our home I was tired, not having slept properly for two nights, terribly hungry, dirty and messy. But I had to forget all these things when I found twenty refugees in the same condition, trying to adjust themselves to a tiny house which had barely provided my wife and myself with living quarters. As the walls for the most part had broken down, and the refugees were single women, single men and married folks, I had to set to and make ways for dividing the house into rooms, which I did by hanging up sheets and table cloths.

I was now running by faith a kind of "refugee" hotel, with tinned goods supplied by an ever seeing, understanding and living God. I arranged for some to do the cooking, others to go and hunt for water, and then I had to make myself a kind of clerk, interviewing each refugee, inquiring whether they had relatives in other sections of Japan or not, and arranging for them to leave the city as quickly as possible. We could not possibly stay very long huddled together in that condition. We were still in the heat of summer; there was no water, no sanitary arrangements; everything was turned upside down by the quake and the very best thing was for every refugee to get out of town and spend some time with their relatives in other cities. The railway company made this possible by supplying free transportation out of Yokohama for refugees.

But I was now facing another hard circumstance. There had been brought to our home a young baby, still a suckling,

THE GREAT JAPANESE EARTHQUAKE 117

a Japanese, but born of British naturalized parents who had been killed in the earthquake. The parents were Christian workers with other missionaries, and the baby had been brought to our home for our care and provision. For two or three days we were able to get a little milk from a cow that we found in Yokohama, but this was taken away from the city the third day. I then realized there was only one way to save the baby's life and that was to make a return journey to Karuizawa with the child.

I begged for a volunteer to accompany me with the baby. A girl of seventeen did so. I obtained her mother's consent and promised her that by the grace and help of God I would do my best to bring her back safely.

The awful atmosphere in Yokohama, the tremendous spiritual depression, the abominable smells of the burning of human flesh everywhere, cannot be fully described. Hundreds, yea thousands of earthquakes caused the ground to reel to and from every few seconds or minutes. The great earthquake had been a tremendous plunge of this part of the globe, and now the earth was receding with hundreds and thousands of smaller quakes. One could not sleep right through the night without being wakened up dozens of times by these smaller quakes.

I started out early one morning with my baby and the young Christian as a nurse. We had just one feeding bottle filled with milk and, of course, that was soon gone. The nipple was lost on the tram and the bottle got smashed. When we finally arrived in the suburbs of Tokyo at nightfall we found that martial law had been declared and all who were out after dark were in danger of being shot down.

I was really in a fix. I had the baby, minus milk, a Japanese girl acting as nurse, and en route another Japanese lady had sought my protection and care. I found a military encampment close at hand and begged the officer in charge to at least take care of my Japanese friends, and I would hide under some hedge during the night hours trusting God to protect me from all danger.

That there was danger there was no doubt. The military

had to exercise every strictness. Profiteers were killed on the spot, and only by immediate action were the authorities able to hold the people and control those who were taking advantage for wrong purposes of the conditions brought about by the earthquake.

I can well understand how strange it must have seemed to the officer of this encampment to see a European, hatless, clothes dirty, with a Japanese baby and two young Japanese women. I could read the doubts going through his mind, so I pled with him to take care of the Japanese party and I would take care of myself. However, he finally agreed for us all to sleep on the ground under a large tent, and again this night became one that will ever live in my memory.

There must have been several hundred of us in that large tent that night sleeping on the straw mats on the ground. An unusually strong earthquake awoke everybody about two o'clock in the morning, and the combined crying of the crowd resounds in my ears today. "We are going to die after all; what shall we do?" Was it any wonder that the title of the first editorial that I wrote for "Japan and Pentecost," after the earthquake, was "The Cries of Damned Souls"? (see a copy of this editorial on a later page).

The next morning we got on our way early as there was no milk for the baby, and our aim was to get it to a place of safety alive. There was no way to wash it or to change its clothes, and no milk to feed it. We did manage to get some water down its throat which, with faith and prayer, helped to keep it alive. We found that a train was being run in the direction we wished to go, but what a time we had! The platform was absolutely packed like sardines in a tin. There was a great deal of confusion as to where the train was going. First we got in the train, then we were told to get out. This happened two or three times until we did not know where we were. The crowds were so tremendous that there were at least ten men on the front of the engine, several on top, and every carriage had dozens of men riding outside as well as being packed inside.

THE GREAT JAPANESE EARTHQUAKE

Finally, I was assured that the train I was in was the right one. The whistle blew and the train began to move, but as it did I noticed my baby and the nurse on the platform outside the train. She had evidently gotten out during the confusion about where the train was to go. I had to act quickly. Opening the window, I called out, "That is my baby, and the girl with it must come with me." Some man caught on to the situation, opened the carriage door, and the girl and the baby were thrown bodily in. Of course, the poor baby was using its lungs to their capacity, as it hit its head on the carriage floor. But praise the Lord, the baby was still alive, and three or four mothers on this train endeavored to nurse the same, and we arrived at Karuizawa in safety. I handed the baby over to the Japan Rescue Mission right away, and with medical care and special attention the baby revived. The child grew up and was trained for the Lord's service.

Just how many days I had been away from my family I do not remember, but it was a considerable number. There was absolutely no means of communication, although I had written one or two notes asking folks that I had met who were going to Karuizawa to carry them to my wife. They had not arrived. On the contrary I was supposed to be dead. For one morning a friend called on my wife and said, "Have you seen the bulletin board today?" The way the question was asked raised doubts in my wife's mind, and she quickly went to see what the bulletin board had to say. Daily reports were being posted of those known to be killed or wounded in the quake, and this particular morning there was a note saying: "Coote has been found dead."

I realized when I arrived at the cottage where the family was that I was untidy; my white clothes were now black. I had been unable to shave for days and days. Water was at a premium for drinking purposes. But I could not understand why my wife seemed slow to recognize me. The simple reason was that she thought I was dead, and it was as if I had come back from the grave.

Similar reports were given to my wife's mother in America, who even said that friends had told them that they had seen my wife and children lying dead in the streets of Yokohama.

My next job was to prepare the family for America. There was no possibility of going back to Yokohama, and as the Red Cross was offering to take refugees back home, I considered the same the wiser plan, so that I might get the mind of the Lord and start afresh in a new city.

I should have said that while arriving at Yokohama practically penniless, first one refugee and then another handed me a few pennies, or two or three yen with the remark, "Teacher Coote, money is useless to us. Take this, it will help out a little." So that I was thus able to get back to Karuizawa. But I was now penniless again, and facing the need of paying the railway fare back to Tokyo for the family.

But God is ever on time. Hallelujah. How wonderfully He works! I did not know it, but in the train journey to Tokyo there happened to be a teacher. We did not speak to each other, but the Lord spoke to him to give me Yen 10.00. I did not know this but he told the story to another missionary this way. "I felt I ought to give Mr. Coote Yen 10.00, but I was a little timid to do so. But though some days have passed I am not comfortable, and feel that I must give him that money. Will you take it to him for me?" We received the money the very day the family went to Tokyo.

But this was not enough. I did not want the children to see the dead bodies lying on the streets, and asked the Lord to give me a little more so that I might get a taxi across Tokyo. This was an unusual request for to hire a taxi in the earthquake time was practically equal to buying one.

Where is the limit of faith? Does not the Word declare "All things are yours?" I was at the station looking over the times of the trains. A missionary there entered into a conversation regarding the earthquake and our losses in the same. He continued, "Well, I suppose you have a reserve fund to draw on in this emergency." When I told him that I did not believe in reserve accounts, but lived from day to day trusting God, he scolded me and said, "That is the

THE GREAT JAPANESE EARTHQUAKE 121

matter with you Pentecostal folks, you do not use common sense." I was in no attitude to discuss with him the pros or the cons for a life of faith, and simply said, "Let us not argue about that now," and walked away. But he called after me and gave me Yen 10.00. Little did he know that he was proving my way to be correct, for had I had a reserve account in the bank it would have been of little use to me at that time. The banks suffered just the same destruction and confusion as other folks did. In fact, the American bank with whom I dealt had all their books burned up in the quake, and only a very few records were saved.

We arrived safely at Tokyo, and were put up at the Imperial Hotel, the finest hotel in Japan. The next morning we had to hurry to catch the American gunboat taking refugees to the American liner sailing for America. I had very little time to say good-bye to my wife, and she left for Seattle with the children without anything, money or clothes. I was in practically the same condition and had a small bill to meet at Karuizawa for I had bidden my wife to go into debt for a little milk for the children, as I felt we could not deprive them of this.

"All things work together for good to them that love God." So says the Word, and our experiences have proved the same to be true over and over again. Imagine my wife's surprise when she found that instead of being placed on a boat heading for America, she was on a liner leaving for China. This seemed to be too much. To arrive in China without a home, without clothes, without money, what a tragedy! But God! Amen and amen. Some Baptist missionaries spontaneously and without my wife's knowledge took up a collection for her. A sailor found out the reason for my wife's tears, arranged for a lifeboat to be swung over the side of the boat, and my wife and family were transferred to another liner heading for America.

The Spirit bade my wife to have the amount of collection sent to me at Karuizawa from Kobe by a postal money order and I, too, was amazed at the receipt of a registered letter as I arrived at Karuizawa again to settle up matters there. I was therefore able to pay my milk bill, settle up the house, and return to Yokohama.

God had made me to know that Oaska was my next post. Having placed most of the refugees at Yokohama, I now headed for Osaka with seven or eight of them. But I could hardly arrive in Osaka without a penny, and so God again opened a door that no man could shut. Praise His holy name.

I met the manager of a bank in Yokohama who wished to get some furniture to start a little office so that he could carry on negotiations in the city. It so happened that I had the things he wanted and could not use them myself, nor could I get them out of town to take to Osaka with me.

He bought these items from me, and I was able to start the next section of the journey by the grace of God, taking with me a number of refugees to Osaka.

FIRST EDITORIAL OF
"JAPAN AND PENTECOST"

AFTER THE GREAT JAPANESE EARTHQUAKE

This editorial is taken from the September, 1923 issue of the "Japan and Pentecost" magazine.

THE CRIES OF THE DAMNED

Every eye-witness of the earthquake, when writing about how it brought the city of Yokohama to ruins in the space of a few seconds, made very special mention of the yells, groans, the terrible screams that rent the air at the first shock from terror striken people.

In direct contrast to such cries of torment were the

THE GREAT JAPANESE EARTHQUAKE   123

testimonies of the spirit baptized souls. Two were in No. 1
Mission at the time of the quake, and they immediately fell
on their knees in prayer, afterwards rescuing neighbors
from beneath beams and other debris.

Not only these yells and screams, but the awful sight of
canals containing dead bodies, and piles of them here and
there bring to us afresh the terrible fact that many hundreds
more of Yokohama's population might have heard and
known the way of life had the Christian Church, and individual members of it, been wisely pouring out its gifts
supporting tent campaigns and native workers.

As I have climbed over debris after debris, and crossed
corpse after corpse the last few days, many deep thoughts
have been mine. Here (Japan) tens of thousands suddenly
ushered into eternity with no hope, no forgiveness of sin
and no change of heart. There (America, England,
Australia), a knowledge of salvation and an open Bible for
years, and luxury; spending money on unnecessary things,
and the few remaining coppers for missions.

But now that the catastrophe is past, what shall we do,
and what becomes our personal duty? In every country
drives are being made to relieve Japan - everywhere
appeals made for clothing, money and other necessities.
And they are coming, thanks to the generosity of the Anglo
Saxon folks.

But does our responsibility stop at merely feeding and
clothing these unfortunates? Are we still going to continue
to overlook our SPIRITUAL DEBT to the millions still
living who know not Jesus? Is our sympathy for their
physical and material needs going to eclipse the crying need
of their spiritual nakedness?

Oh, that the news of this earthquake might shake
hundreds of young men and women from their sleep of
slothfulness, and send them to these shores as flaming
evangelists of an apostolic gospel!

Are we going to read accounts of dead corpses piled up
by the hundreds in the streets in Japan, and then continue
to hoard up our means in banks instead of pouring it

through Holy Ghost channels to bring light and salvation to the people of Osaka?

Japan is a country of vast destructive fires and earthquakes. Who can tell what another year will bring to the city of Osaka with its 3,000,000 inhabitants? "Earthquakes in divers places," the Word says. It may be Osaka's turn next. The blood of her heathen souls should weigh heavily upon you - you have the gospel, they have not. It is imperative that you do what you can now.

OSAKA CASTLE

CHAPTER FIFTEEN

CITY OF OSAKA

*"Arise, go to Ninevah, that great city, and cry against it,
for their wickedness is come up before me."*
(Jonah 1:2)

I shall never forget the first house in which I lived in this huge metropolis of Osaka. My friends in the homeland did not know how to get in touch with me, and what funds I had were very small, and yet I had a number of refugees, so had to rent a rather large house to accommodate us all.

And I wished to do this near to where we would be doing evangelistic work to save street car fares. Eventually I found a cheap house near the slums, and because of the low level of the ground the house practically floated when it rained. Here for months I made soap boxes do for desks, chairs, and everything else. I slept on the floor, and the rats had a grand time running up and down my body during the night, and it should be an easy matter to put out my hand in the morning and catch a rat running by.

Within sixty days of the great earthquake I had rented a mission hall on the street leading to the Tobita licensed prostitution quarters which hold 1,500 licensed prostitutes. Here we started an every night campaign, and sometimes we would fill the hall holding 200 people twice a night.

Men of every class and description found the Lord. Sinners of every hue and color were among the penitents. I shall never forget one evening after all the rest had left the building a tall, well built young man stayed behind. He told a story the like of which I had never heard. His list of sins made every one's eyes to blink with surprise. Even that night he was waiting for the clock to strike a certain hour when he would meet other members of his gang and break into a certain rich man's house in the neighborhood.

Harlots, concubines, prostitutes, drunkards, gamblers, housebreakers -- what a motly crowd we had for a congregation. Sometimes the crowds would stand by us loyally. Other nights, just a word wrongly placed in the message would cause one to leave the hall, and the rest would all follow suit, and by the middle of the sermon, there would not be a soul left, although the place was packed with 200 people a few minutes before.

Souls were saved, baptized in water, and in the Holy Ghost. As a result, the Ichioka Church was opened, then Haginochyaya Church was opened. (This later had to be closed for financial reasons.) Then Tamatsukuri Church was opened. This has now become independent and is under the direction of two of our converts. Again Sakae Church was opened. In other words, men from all parts of Osaka, who came to this locality for their pleasure, when they were saved, wished for a place of worship in their neighborhood.

The district became stirred. We had entered the lions' den. Not only were we on the street where 1,500 girls were held in slavery, but the whole district was more or less connected with the same business. Our preaching therefore brought conviction to the neighbors, but they could not give up their business connection, so they banded together to have us ousted. This was finally accomplished, but not without a fight on our part. They took us to court, but as we had a lease for one year, the judge gave us the decision. In court, we had an opportunity to give a gospel witness. Asked for what purpose we used the building, I expained the whole gospel from the life of Christ. But when the lease was ended, we had to leave the building, which was then turned into a skating rink, which failed.

Osaka is a city of three million souls. A later chapter will describe the Osaka Evangelistic Tabernacle, which God graciously has given to us since the end of the Pacific War. It is located almost within two blocks of the Mission Hall mentioned in this chapter.

CHAPTER SIXTEEN
IKOMA BIBLE SCHOOL

"And the things that thou hast heard of me among many
witnesses, the same commit thou to faithful men;
who shall be able to teach others also."
(2 Timothy 2:2)

During the Yokohama revival it was gradually dawning on us that the Lord did not wish us to continue our efforts in Yokohama. It was brought strongly to our hearts that the call of God was "Japan and Pentecost," meaning we were to have a ministry throughout the whole of Japan, and for this reason it was important to train men and women who would take the responsibility of evangelizing their own people.

Even before the Yokohama earthquake, God had enabled us to see many baptized in the Holy Ghost in various prefectures including the city of Kobe in Hyogo prefecture, the city of Osaka in the Osaka prefecture, the city of Yokohama in the Kanagawa prefecture, the city of Tokyo in the Tokyo prefecture, besides the town of Koga in the Ibaraki prefecture, and points in Tochigi prefecture.

Though gradually at first, the scriptural plan of "A Self Supporting, Self Governing, and Self Propagating church" was being deeply impressed on our minds.

Even before the Yokohama earthquake a number of young men had offered their lives to the work of the ministry, and we were having regular morning Bible studies for them. One of the last acts before the earthquake was the renting of a fairly large building for the Bible School in Yokohama to be started in the fall of the earthquake year.

But when the first shocks of the great disaster and the losses entailed were overcome, and with the leading of God to make our headquarters in Osaka, we realized more than ever that God was leading us to a wider mission for the work in Japan. My wife and family returned from America the February following the earthquake and our first two missionaries, Mona Jackson (now Mrs. Adolph Richert), and Miss Fuselier came to us from America.

Not having any confirmation from God as to what He was going to do, but simply feeling the great need for a training school for workers, and the necessity of building a suitable place, my wife and I worked out plans for the same. We tried to make these as economical as possible, and finally asked a contractor for his ideas and prices, and were so shocked at the cost, we shelved the plans and gave the matter up as absolutely impossible as far as we were concerned.

But there cannot be the slightest doubt that God was moving in ways we were not aware. Returning to Osaka on September 1, 1924, the first anniversary of the great earthquake, I was on my way to the post office to collect my mail.

Knowing a ship had recently arrived from America, I thought possibly there might be some mail for us. I was about a block and a half from the post office when a voice spoke quietly to me: "What would you do if there was a check for $1,000 in the mail?" Thinking the voice was from the evil one to try to make me puffed up, I pled the blood of Jesus against it, and continued my journey to the post office.

I received my mail, and was looking over it, when a clerk called me, "Wait Mr. Coote, there is a specially insured letter for you." It was from the great friend of missionaries, George B. Studd of Los Angeles. In it he wrote remarks to the following effect: "Brother Coote, have you been praying specially about something lately? A certain lady in the mission here told me she had an offering for you. I knew she did not enjoy much of this world's goods, so thought it would be at the most just a very few dollars. While I was dealing with some people at the altar Sunday night she came to me, placed a slip of paper in my hand saying, 'This is for Leonard Coote in Japan.' I placed it in my pocket, and was shocked on returning home to find that it was ONE

IKOMA BIBLE SCHOOL 129

THOUSAND DOLLARS!" Dear reader, this check was so timed by the Lord that it arrived on the very first anniversary of the great earthquake, and just after my wife and I, through lack of faith, had placed to one side the plans we had for the building of the Bible School.

Some people have called me the "long headed Englishman" because I want to always be sure of a new move from God. If ever I wanted to be absolutely positive of God's will, it was regarding this school. I confided the matter to my wife, and we decided not to write about it to anyone for some time. We placed the money in the bank for God to give us another indisputable witness if He wanted it used for the Bible School.

The next witness came through an offering from a stranger who lived in London. Apparently I was not a stranger to him, as he had supplied oil to the firm for which I had worked five years in Kobe, and he had heard of my evangelistic activities. The Lord witnessed to us that the offering was for the building of the Bible School and the money was deposited with the first amount, and a simple statement made in our magazine, "Japan and Pentecost" that God was leading regarding the school.

The first requirement now was to know God's will and plan for the location. After a good deal of prayer, we felt led to employ temporarily, a young man who needed financial help, to scout out all the suburban districts around the city of Osaka. Likely spots we also visited, praying for God to guide. No witness came as we investigated place after place, but when we went to Ikoma and inspected the present site, the witness of the Spirit was overwhelming, and the lots of about three acres came to about the combined amount of the two offerings just mentioned.

Two further witnesses settled once and for all the will of God concerning the Bible School and the site we had chosen. I was reading an old copy of the magazine "The Japan Evangelist" in a friend's home, and read an article entitled: "The Hunger Map of Japan" showing that the prefecture of Nara (where the Ikoma Bible School is located) had a lesser amount of Christian work, a lesser number of Christian workers and missionaries than any other prefecture in the whole of the Japanese empire! Oh how wonderfully God had guided! He had led us to center our efforts in the most needy spot in the whole of Japan, yet it was in close proximity to the city of Osaka with its three million people, and the city of Kyoto within an hour's train ride, besides hundreds of other cities, towns and villages waiting for the gospel in every direction!

The other witness concerned the holding of property by Europeans in Japan. Hitherto foreigners could not hold property in their own name. About the time of the purchase of the site of the Ikoma Bible School, a new law was passed enabling Britishers to purchase and to hold land in their own names. Again we traced the leading of the mighty hand of the God of Abraham, and Isaac and of Jacob!

Having seen such wonderful manifestations of God's leading, the supply of finances for the land and the location, I expected God would immediately send in the necessary funds for the building of the school itself. But months went by, and nothing more came in. More months went by, and only a little came in to pay for the taxes and necessary expenses in holding the property. Doubts began to arise; sneers from some in Japan were hurled at the waiting property, and unbelief was doing its best to destroy the work that God had already undertaken.

How slow we human beings are to believe the Lord! How easily we are led to discouragement and doubts by outward circumstances! How little do we justify the Lord, and through every circumstance declare to the three worlds, the world of fallen spirits, the earth itself, and heaven, that God is faithful; that He cannot fail, and that if He sees fit to have us wait, He is all wise and cannot err.

I was greatly perplexed because God had so wonderfully guided up to the present, and now we had come to a total standstill. Not that God was not constantly granting us manifestations of His power and grace along other lines, for

IKOMA BIBLE SCHOOL

it was at this time that we received two cables in the same month, one sending funds for the starting of the printing department, (more of which will be mentioned in a later chapter), and the second cable for the purchase of a new tent for evangelism.

At this time, a brother from Canada wrote a letter that deeply impressed me. It said, "Brother Coote, take your Bible to the compound ground and open it at Mark 1:23:

"For verily I say unto you, that whosoever shall say unto this mountain, be thou removed, and be thou cast into the sea; and shall not doubt in his heart, but shall believe that those things which he saith shall come to pass, he shall have whatsoever he saith."

Kneel down on the compound ground; claim this promise and God will work for you." It was only a little while before the Lord showed very definitely to us that I should visit America, and during this trip the Lord miraculously supplied for the building of the Bible School.

MISSIONARY HOME ON CAMPUS

CHAPTER SEVENTEEN

FIRST TIME LEAVING JAPAN

"i will instruct thee and teach thee in the way
which thou shalt go; I will guide
thee with mine eye."
(Psalm 32:8)

Engaging in missionary work right after leaving business, and continuing the same for a period of eleven years, (totaling sixteen years of unbroken residence in Japan), the point had often been raised as to whether I ought or ought not to make a visit to Canada and America, visiting the assemblies, and becoming better acquainted with Pentecostal work as a whole. It should be remembered that though I had labored along Pentecostal lines for upwards of eleven years I had never visited any Pentecostal work in my own language, and the only white workers that I had met were the missionaries in Japan, or those passing through from China. Discouragements had been many, and I was not yet able to understand the reason for God's silence regarding the Bible School. Some misunderstandings had arisen in America regarding my methods, and purposes, and on the whole it was generally considered that a visit to America, and a period out of Japan, would be beneficial physically, as well as spiritually. But while these advantages were granted in principle, the will of the Lord was not definitely known, and there had been no provision made financially for such a visit. The matter was urgently laid on my heart one day, and as some missionaries had returned to the homeland we had a surplus of furniture, and I put the matter to a test. If God really desired that I should make the visit home, He would enable me to sell the furniture. Ordinarily there would not be any possibility of selling it, but God was leading, and enough was realized to pay my third class travelling across the Pacific Ocean.

I arrived in Vancouver Christmas day knowing nobody.

FIRST TIME LEAVING JAPAN 133

It was a dreadfully rainy day. I knew no one in the city, and was really afraid to meet anyone. I was quite nervous, and having been so long in Japan without a break, it was difficult to become accustomed to large numbers of Europeans. I shall never forget the sentiment that came over me as the Empress liner gradually came into the docks. Hundreds of faces of Canadians peered from off the pier. I had not seen such a large number of white men at one time for sixteen years, and felt embarrassed moving among them. There was another lady on board who had been in Japan for a long time, and as the boat drew near, to the amusement of other passengers she cried out "What a lot of foreigners!" (Europeans naturally being aliens in Japan are called foreigners by Westerners and Japanese alike).

I located myself in a hotel near the pier, and after resting a little, it came to me that an address of a mission that I had at New Westminster was not very far away. After telephoning, I managed to get to the meeting and was asked to speak. This I could not do. I would gladly have done so if it had been in Japanese, but for two or three days I walked the streets speaking to everybody and my English began to return, and gradually I found how to address an audience in the English language.

I spent a few days in this hotel waiting on the Lord, and was considering seeking temporary employment while seeking physical rest and uplift, intending to return to Japan in three months.

But God had other plans. After my message at the Pyramid Temple in Vancouver one evening, a lady came to me and informed me that her mother had left a little money some years ago, which she in turn gave back to God for Him to use as He desired. Many Christian efforts requiring funds, and home and foreign missionaries had been met and their pleas heard, but God had never led to the using of this money. The lady explained that while I was ministering God had made it clear that Ikoma Bible College was the object for the use of this money. I thus received my first offering for the same: two hundred dollars.

134 IMPOSSIBILITIES BECOME CHALLENGES

As doors began to open for my testimony, the Lord revealed to me that I was not to work with my hands, but to speak of the needs of Japan wherever the opportunity was granted. Further, the Lord asked me to do this in a particular way. I was to go wherever I was invited, but I was to refuse offerings for the work, trusting God entirely for the expenses en route, the support of the work in Japan, and for the amount necessary for the building of the Bible School.

My wife had gladly consented to stay in Japan during my absence, to keep the work going, trusting God for the funds for her own living, the support of six or seven missions and as many national workers. What this meant will be understood when I say that, of the seven rents payable, one of them amounted to $100.00 gold.

I astonished various pastors and evangelists when I informed them of my stand financially. Over and over I was told that it could not be done. Others told me the people would take advantage of my desiring no offering and that I would be stranded. I felt the call of God upon my heart to take this stand, and I am sure the results prove that it was of God. I should say that reading the manner of Hudson Taylor's visit to the homelands caused me in some measure to feel this was the right course to adopt.

On two occasions, in the cities of Seattle and Oakland, I had cause to prove that my method was right. In stating to the pastors in charge, one of them said, "I know Brother Coote that you are not asking for offerings. I appreciate that, but I am taking the offering, and not you". In that case the pastor told the people to throw their money on to the platform, and I was thus forced to accept the same. But the following Sunday being asked to preach in the same place again, I stipulated that I would if there was no mention made whatsoever about money. This was agreed on and I was able to inform the pastor that I received a greater amount financially for the work of God in Japan when no mention was made in any shape or form of collection than when my hand was forced and out of the deep love of the pastor's heart he had the people bring the gifts to the

FIRST TIME LEAVING JAPAN

platform.

In the other case I was preaching three or four nights consecutively. The last night was Sunday. I had mentioned my stand to the pastor, but he felt he would not be doing his duty towards me if no offering were taken. I insisted that a collection be taken up for the needs of the local work, that no mention be made of my need or the work in Japan, but let God have His way. I saw the pastor was a little troubled that I might not receive anything, and that I would suffer for lack of expenses. I assured him saying, "Brother pastor, let me ask you a question. Supposing I granted you the privilege of taking an offering for me tonight, just about how much would you receive in the offering?" "Well," he replied, "as you are a returning missionary and not one going out to the field, your offering would be rather small, but I suppose you would receive $25.00." I then said, "Now look here. You take up the regular offering for the rent, lights and needs of the work here tonight, and leave me with the Lord. I will call tomorrow morning and I am sure you will get a better collection than usual for your own needs, and I am going to believe God that I will receive even more than what you think I would receive if you took an offering". "All right," he said, and the next morning I called to say good-bye. The pastor was truly amazed when I told him that I had received as much as $40, and he had received the regular offering for the local needs in addition.

God enabled me to hold to this principle, as I extended my visit from three months to one whole year. I was able to travel and preach throughout the states of Washington, Oregon, Idaho, California, New Mexico, Indiana, Oklahoma, Texas, Louisiana, Arkansas, Missouri, Ohio, Maryland, and New York. In fact, there was only one or, at the most, two or three states in the Union that I did not visit. In the majority of cases, I stayed at Y.M.C.A.s, paying my own hotel expenses, food and travel. I refused offerings for the work, for myself, or even for traveling expenses. God abundantly supplied every need.

Some rather remarkable incidents took place showing the way God caused people to supply my needs. In one

136   **IMPOSSIBILITIES BECOME CHALLENGES**

case a lady left the meeting and returned home but did not have any peace in her soul until she returned to the mission and placed a five dollar bill in my hand.

I was asked to speak on an only night I had open at a small town in the southern oil fields. In order to do this I had to travel all day, arriving at the town hardly an hour before the meeting, and leave again the next morning very early. I was only able to give a testimony to what God had done in Japan and desired to do. Before catching the early morning train, a lady had to obey the Lord and bring $200 in cash for the building of the Ikoma Bible College.

At a small mission in Washington, I gave three or four meetings. One of the prominent brothers in the mission, a hard working carpenter, grasped me by the hand at the beginning of the meetings and told me that he was afraid for me, thinking that I had gotten too big ideas and was getting away from God in desiring to build a Bible School in Japan.

My reply was, "Brother, I will not say anything. Just let God talk in these meetings, and see how you feel about it then." He came to me the last day of the meetings and, with tears in his eyes, asked me to forgive him for opposing the Bible School proposition, for God had now shown him that this was His will, and as a proof He handed me the last $100.00 he possessed towards the building of the same.

In order to prove God to the very utmost, whenever I received funds, I would have them deposited in a bank awaiting my return to Japan. I would allow a very small amount for my expenses in getting to the next appointment, trusting the Lord in the meantime to supply further for the next town. At one place in California, I had spent all the cash I had to get to the town, and I did later receive a small check, but had not the cash to get out of town. Ignorant of my circumstances (of course I had funds in the bank, but none in my pocket allowed for traveling expenses, as I had received nothing during the meetings in this town) the pastor at the last moment offered to drive me to my next appointment and God thus again supplied my needs.

FIRST TIME LEAVING JAPAN

Amen. As I drew nearer and nearer the eastern coast, it came to me that I should seek the mind of the Lord regarding a hasty visit across the Atlantic to see my father and mother again after sixteen years separation. I was seeking the mind of the Lord regarding this matter when a pastor confirmed the question as being of God and I was able to spend just two or three weeks in England. I was determined to be very careful in knowing the mind of the Lord. The boat left for England about nine in the evening, and I well remember how I prayed almost every hour of that afternoon to be definitely guided by the Lord in taking this further step. The shipping clerk thought I was a little strange in not being able to give a definite reply until an hour or so before the sailing of the boat, but I had proven it pays to make very sure of the will of the Lord in all matters.

As I was due to be back in time for the New Year's Convention, I felt that the visit to England was not for a preaching tour, but just to do honor to my father and mother whom I had not seen for so many years. I knew, however, that it would be hard to resist all influences brought to bear on me to stay longer, so decided on a very short stay, and cabled the information from the boat. I also decided not to preach anywhere but to give the whole of the very short time to my parents.

I was compelled, however, on account of shipping regulations to spend a day or so in London, and being pressed I did give way and spoke at one place twice, but only on the same conditions as those laid down in America.

Whatever doubts there might have remained in my mind as to whether it was right or otherwise to make the Atlantic trip were more than swept away when the pastor of the aforementioned place gave me an offering covering the entire cost of the return fare from New York to Southampton and other expenses.

I made the return journey chiefly through Canada, observing the same rule as followed in America, and was able to arrive back at my starting place, Vancouver, testifying that God had taken me across the whole continent,

138   IMPOSSIBILITIES BECOME CHALLENGES

across the Atlantic Ocean and back, and right through the Canadian continent, without my having to beg a single penny, being able to refuse all offerings and collections, send a little money to Japan, and have in hand a surplus of $4,000.00 for the building of the Ikoma Bible School.

But I had considered $5,000.00 would be necessary for this building. I reasoned if God was able supply $4,000.00, He was just as able to supply the remaining $1,000.00. I made a hurried visit to Seattle to have a farewell meeting with my wife's relatives before sailing again for Japan. My preaching engagements were really finished, and I was pretty well tired, having traveled night and day, speaking oftentimes twice a day, besides controlling the work in Japan by correspondence, and editing "Japan and Pentecost" as well.

However, I was asked to speak in a couple of rescue missions in Seattle before sailing. Rather reluctantly, I agreed. A lady, unknown to me, and I fully believe I was unknown to her, arrived at the first mission after I had begun to speak, so she did not even know my name, and knew nothing of where I was staying. During my message the Lord spoke very definitely to her to give me for the work that I was doing in Japan $1,000.00 that she had in the bank. Of course I had no knowledge of this, but she herself told me later how she went home, and the next day gathered some of her friends together to pray for confirmation of the leading as well as for information as to where I could be reached.

Well, I do remember the next night. The mission at which I was to speak had just removed to a new location and had not yet gotten properly settled. I was very, very tired, and on account of the very poor attendance, really wondered whether I had made a mistake in consenting to speak. Just before the meeting started, however, this lady--a complete stranger to me--handed me an envelope which contained a check for $1,000.00 for the building of the Bible School.

How my praises ascended up to the great God who had

FIRST TIME LEAVING JAPAN

started me off just a year before in the city of Vancouver to trust Him without offerings for the $5,000 required for the building of the Ikoma Bible College. Here I was in Seattle with all preaching appointments finished, having traveled throughout America, over the Atlantic, across Canada, and now back in Seattle sailing within a few days for Japan, and in a small rescue mission the Lord graciously placed in my hand the last $1,000.00 to fulfil His leading and His Word. Oh! That we Christians might learn to trust Him more fully!

COOTE FAMILY - 1937

CHAPTER EIGHTEEN

IN THE LIONS' DEN

"When thou passest through the waters, I will be with thee; and through the rivers, they shall not overflow thee: when thou walkest through the fire, thou shalt not be burned; neither shall the flame kindle upon thee."
(Isaiah 43:2)

No one can fully estimate how happy I was when God so remarkably supplied the needs for the building of the Bible School. Again forward steps were taken for the fulfillment of the God given call of "Japan and Pentecost until Jesus comes."

Sisters Lye and Stromquist had accompanied me back to Japan. These new missionaries were soon followed by Brother and Sister Richert; later by Brother and Sister Glaeser.

It was not long before the campus took on a different appearance; foundations were laid, and eventually the framework of the Bible School went up. During the summer preceding the opening of the school, God enabled us to pitch the tent in a very central location in the city of Kyoto, enlarging it until it held 800 people, and we had a wonderful time. Brother Johnson who had been with the work during my absence and Brother Clover, who came over specially for a summer's tent work, united together and a good campaign was held.

Eventually the Bible School was formally opened, representatives from the Ikoma Primary School, Post Office, Police, and Municipal authorities gathering together to celebrate its opening. The mayor of Ikoma sent a special letter of congratulations to be read by a special messenger. The opening and dedication services attended by missionaries of other bodies all tended to show a mighty move forward in the evangelization of Nara prefecture, and

IN THE LION'S DEN   141

later throughout the length and breadth of Japan.

Twenty young men and women entered the school. Right away tent campaigns were arranged for the untouched and unreached territories of this heathen prefecture of Nara.

We had seen and felt the opposition of the enemy just as soon as God began to supply the needs for the building, but we did not realize the depth and length to which the enemy would go in order to destroy the work that God had started. While I was still in America a storm had broken through our ground, destroying a considerable portion, and the heavy waters had raged to the neighboring field destroying rice crops, and this neighbor now held us responsible for damages, so that on my return from the U.S.A. I was faced first with this claim for damages. But God wonderfully overruled and what seemed to be at first a disaster turned out to our good for in lieu of damages our neighbor finally agreed to accept our purchase of his land and so our ground was far increased in size.

But the real nature of the enemy was revealed when all arrangements had been made for a tent campaign in the city of Koriyama, in Nara prefecture, a place with 20,000 people situated close to Ikoma. This city possessed two licensed prostitution quarters, and is built upon lust and liquor, a terrible foundation for a city. And we were to know something of the powers of these forces when they were stirred, and set against us.

The routine matters had been followed in receiving police permission for the tent campaigns, and the ground had been rented to us by the municipal authorities themselves so there was nothing to worry about in this respect. The tent meeting opened with victory, and quickly souls were being brought under mighty conviction. Men and women were seeking God, and some were getting right through. Then about the fourth day, after I had taught in the Bible School in the morning, I found a telegram on my desk reading, "Take your tent down right away today," signed by the municipal authorities.

No reason for this change of mind was given, and though a special visit was made to inquire, no reason was given to us. Finally, however, we found out that the owners of the licensed prostitution quarters had protested to the municipal authorities about loaning us the ground, and as some of the keepers of these brothels are on the council itself, they simply had to ask us to stop the meeting.

It was not long after this that I was called to the local police office. Behind closed doors I was quizzed again and again. I was accused of opening the Bible School secretly and of doing spiritual work without the permission of the authorities. All these accusations were really ridiculous for papers had been filed with the authorities and the police themselves were our guests at the opening service. At first I was completely taken aback, and was tremendously bewildered. These interviews became more and more frequent. The accusations were more and more serious. Doubts were raised that I was using the Bible School as a sort of training ground for Communists, and even deportation of myself and family was mentioned in the interviews.

One day right in my presence my very words were turned around, and a report by telephone was given just to the opposite of what I had said. It came to me right there and then that I had stirred up a hornet's nest, and that I had now all the wolves and dogs of the spiritual under-world on my track, and only God could rescue me from the lions' den.

After consultations with Japanese and missionary friends I found it advisable to humble myself on every occasion before the police authorities; do exactly what they bade me to do, for it was evident that our enemies, the licensed prostitution quarters and heathenism had banded together, and were seeking every possible loophole through minor technical points of the law to have us ousted from our God given position in Ikoma.

Finally one day a crisis came when a police officer brought an order to the school that we must close down right away. I was teaching at the time, and there was noth-

IN THE LION'S DEN

ing else to do but to dismiss the classes, and obey the higher authorities. We considered it wise to wait on the Lord, and let Him work out this matter for us, simply meeting together on Sunday mornings for worship, in various homes, a sort of cottage meeting.

After two or three weeks, I was again taken to the police station, and accused of breaking the law by holding these cottage meetings. Apologies were made, and after more prayer we decided for a time at least to transfer our efforts to the city of Osaka, renting a house temporarily for the housing of the students.

My instruction now from the higher authorities was that I was not allowed to teach or preach in the name of Jesus in the whole of Nara prefecture. Praise the Lord this sounds a little like what is written in the Acts of the Apostles, and if we are to believe God for Apostolic results, it is only natural that we are to expect Apostolic persecution.

One day I found Ikoma all placarded up with bills calling Coote a pig, a dog, and other various and unkind names. I managed to save one of these placards as a momento of these crucial times.

I wish to say, too, that right at this time God saw fit to allow us to go through a very severe financial test, probably the severest we have ever known in the work. Whether God felt after the great victory won through the building of the Bible School that we needed this test, or whether friends generally felt that as we had been able to pray in funds for the school we now did not need their cooperation, I cannot say, but a test, severe in nature and prolonged in time, was added to the already trying circumstances.

I came to the end of the month and found I had $50.00 (ten pounds), insufficient to meet the needs of the work. The principle of the work is "no debts" and hitherto God had always miraculously supplied, even at the last minute every need was met. Special prayer and fasting was resorted to, only to find that at the close of the following month we were $100.00 (twenty pounds) behind. How the enemy used these things to try to discourage! I can hear

144   IMPOSSIBILITIES BECOME CHALLENGES

him now. "Coote, Bible School closed; you are refused permission to teach or preach in this prefecture; debts rising; you are a poor missionary, are you not?" Such was the stern fight the enemy waged, both materially and mentally.

Drastic action had to be taken. All out going funds were closely watched; rigid economy was exercised, and apart from the purchase of rice, no expenditure was permitted for other food, the missionaries all agreeing together to live on whatever was in the house until God undertook. This continued for three months until our bodies simply cried out for milk, for fish and for vegetables; yet God had not yet undertaken. Rather the reverse. The debt had grown from $100 to almost $1,000 (twenty pounds to two hundred pounds).

While the test was prolonged we endeavored with all the grace that God would bestow to encourage ourselves in Him. We realized that God was testing us, for again and again registered letters would arrive without a penny in them. Then a certain lady wrote asking if we had received an offering of $400 she had sent some weeks previously. This was tantalizing indeed. Later this lady was able to receive a duplicate check from the bank and then felt led to send the money elsewhere. Surely such incidents and experiences test one's whole hearted consecration to the Lord! And so the test continued.

Having all the students together in Osaka we pitched a tent campaign there. Our enemies transferred their efforts and opposition to Osaka, and though there was no connection between Ikoma and Osaka, as we had enjoyed full government permission and police protection for years for the work in this city, it was evident we were going to face more work of the enemy. I remember one night saying to one of the workers as I entered the tent, "It is either revival or persecution. I feel it in the air."

I was not mistaken. The tent was crowded to capacity. The crowd was waiting for something; there was a spirit of expectancy. A couple of our students whispered at the

IN THE LION'S DEN

close of the meeting, "Teacher, be careful tonight, there are some men determined to set upon you." I left the tent secretly, but went right into a band of men who were waiting for me on the outside. And what a band of ruffians! One took my right hand, and another my left, and marching me down a dark street, handled me roughly. I maintained an attitude of complete silence, praying and trusting God. Eventually I was released.

The second night a similar occurrence took place, although this time I was protected by a bodyguard of our own students. The ruffians broke through, a number of the students being molested, and again I was taken to a dark street, and badly treated.

My maintaining a silent attitude wore my persecutors out so that after a time they let me go again, but the effect on my nerves was tremendous. I was advised by my workers the third night not to preach, but I felt this was giving way to the enemy, and trusting God I preached but did not leave the tent. After the ordinary meeting had closed, the leader of the ruffians took charge of the congregation, exhorted the crowd to kill me, and at a given signal they all jumped on the seats smashing them and again the mob marched me off down a back alley to a dark lonely place. This time they told me they determined to stay with me right until morning, until I apologized for preaching. They found fault with my message and argued that I was making the Koreans to appear as bad men. I did not say one word, keeping my mouth perfectly tight all the time.

I was so weak this night, and my nerves so taut that I was hardly able to stand, and sat on the dirt ground. During the march the leader had given me a hit on the face with his clenched fist, and I had been kicked in the back. And I knew I could not stand much more physically. Quite a time passed and the persecutors did their utmost to get me to talk. Their object was to instigate a quarrel so that the police would finally have to come and intercept, and so give us a bad name.

146 IMPOSSIBILITIES BECOME CHALLENGES

While they talked murder there was no reason for violence although when they were stirred, being beside themselves, they did things without controlling their actions.

Suddenly the Spirit of God came upon me as I sat on the ground, and I felt impressed to stand up, make one dash through the persecutors' legs, and run. If this were in the natural it would have utterly failed, for I was weak, and my persecutors were many in number, and I was just one. Beside this, the fact of my changed attitude would add fuel to their emotions. At the same time I felt distinctly led to do this. I did it. With all the strength I had I broke through my persecutors' legs and ran. I had not gone more than twenty yards when an arm of one of the believers grasped my back, swinging me around, and helping me go ahead. Then, without any premeditation or consultation, instinctively we both turned around and shouted. It was a shout of triumph. We were only two, but the shout God gave us was such a one as sounded like that of an army. You should have seen our persecutors flee for their lives.

The next day the police intervened. We closed the tent for two or three days rest and God worked out matters. The leader of the ruffians was deported to Korea, and we were permitted to go on with our work.

But imagine if you will the other side of the situation. Returning home again and again with necktie torn away, shirt torn, coat stripped off my back, dishevelled hair, was enough to give a scare to my wife. She did not know when I might be brought home dead. Murder was in the air.

Bible School was still closed. The police instructions that I was not allowed to preach or teach in the prefecture of Nara still held good. Financial tests continued leaving a debt of $1,000 (two hundred pounds) over our heads. Opposing bills placarded on the streets of Ikoma; the tent and equipment virtually destroyed by the ruffians; actual threats of murder; my body molested again and again; surely, this was a test indeed. And then one evening, without any previous sign of sickness, God permitted Mary

IN THE LION'S DEN
147

Anna, our fourth child, to leave this world. What a shock to
us all! We have never been able to fully understand the
reason for the sudden illness, and the cause of the death of
Mary Anna. Even the doctor was reserved in signing the
death statement. It has been felt that poison was brought
into the home and placed on a piece of bread laid on the
floor.

*"All things work together for good, to them that love
God" (Romans 8:28).*

This is hard to believe sometimes, but God's Word declares
it so and there is not the slightest doubt about it.

One morning, when the burden of everything was too
heavy for me to bear, I remember going into one of the
upstairs rooms of the Bible School, and flinging myself
down on the floor before God. I simply cried, "I have come
to an end of everything, I have sought your face, prayed,
fasted, and in spite of every circumstance, believed. But I
cannot go an inch further." I was desperate. And then I
seemed to hear a voice, and the voice said, "Coote, are you
willing to be a failure?" A failure? "Why," I thought, "that
is the very thing that I have been fighting against." I seemed
to see myself in the U.S.A. on various platforms pleading
with God's people to make the Bible School a reality. I
could also visualize the tears of some as they gladly took
out the last hundred dollars from the bank for the building
of this school, and now to have it closed. What could I say?
And then for the Lord to ask me if I was willing to be a
failure. Questions of being deported from Japan were still
in the air. Could this be the will of the Lord? And then the
second time the same voice and identically the same question was heard, "Coote, are you willing to be a failure?"
The emphasis was on the word "willing".

With the repeated question came a revelation from God
that it was not God asking me to be a failure, but whether I
was willing to be a failure. It was a question of full
surrender to anything and everything that God might
choose to allow. Was I willing to be deported? Was I willing for the Bible School to be closed? Was I willing to be

148 IMPOSSIBILITIES BECOME CHALLENGES

murdered? Was I willing to have debts arising to thousands of dollars?

My soul caught the point, and immediately I responded, "Yes, Lord, I am willing. The responsibility is thine, not mine. All I have to do is to surrender." And what a peace came over my soul! I believe I am right in saying that I did not then care if the debt was ten times the size. What mattered if God was on the throne! With this easy, care free condition, I rose from the floor and, singing, I came down the stairs. As I did so, Brother Randall had just entered the Bible School and said, "Brother Coote, there is nothing in the mail this morning." But what did I care? I had the victory now. I looked over some advertisements that had come in the mail and noticed a letter from my brother in England. In it he told me he was asked by a mission near London to give a missionary talk. Being employed and unable to get away from the office he first declined, but finally yielded to pressure. He was given a check for the work of God in Japan, and into my hands fell out from his letter a draft for eighty pounds. Praise be unto God.

Later God led me to lay the matter of the Ikoma Bible School before the British consul, and it was a happy day when the Governor of the Nara prefecture sent around five men to inspect the Bible School premises, as well as to apologize to me for all the trouble that I had received at the hands of the local police. Special permits were given for the school to open, as well as for myself as principal, and a twenty percent reduction of the price of tickets on the Imperial Government Railways for all students and teachers. A thousand times I said, "And the iron did swim!"

It is interesting to look on these incidents and to note how God protects His own and how those who are servants of the enemy suffer loss. It was not long after this that the police detective who gave me the most trouble found his wife strangled by her own hands in the bathroom.

And so the story of "Japan and Pentecost Until Jesus Comes" develops: God leading as to where the Gospel is to

IN THE LION'S DEN

be preached; providing the necessary finances for the support of the work and also producing persecution that would endanger the lives of those engaged in such work, God Himself coming to the rescue and proving Himself to be as the Scripture professes,

"I will never leave thee nor forsake thee,"

and,

"Lo, I am with you always, even unto the end of the world."

CHAPTER NINETEEN

PROBLEMS MET AND OVERCOME

"Think it not strange concerning the fiery trial
which is to try you, as though some
strange thing happened to you."
(1 Peter 4:12)

Our last chapter ended with the victory gained over the intense persecutions that God had permitted to come our way concerning the Ikoma Bible School. The length of these persecutions coupled with the terrible financial test had been a constant strain on all concerned, and while all rejoiced in the blessed victory God had given whereby the Bible School was again opened with full Government permission, and in addition reductions granted on all railway lines for both student and teachers, this victory was overshadowed by the loss of Mary Anna, our fourth child, incidentally referred to in the previous chapter.

It happened all so suddenly that the shock was the greater to all concerned. I had returned rather late that day for my supper, and while I was eating, my wife and one of our missionaries were talking together in another room. Mary Anna was in the room with them. She was in a playful attitude, even singing spiritual choruses, when I was suddenly called into the bedroom. Mary Anna had taken suddenly ill. I prayed and God answered immediately. Mary Anna vomited and seemingly recovered from her sickness. I returned to finish my meal. In a few moments I was called again, and this time a real battle ensued. Mary Anna went into spasms. Japanese workers were called in, and special prayer was offered, all hanging on to God for her recovery. After the Japanese workers had retired for the night, my wife and I sat up alone with the child, and at a few minutes until midnight the Lord saw fit to take her young life back to Himself.

A doctor examined Mary Anna the next morning but

PROBLEMS MET AND OVERCOME 151

made no remarks. Whether the child ate something that disagreed with her, or whether the enemy in some other way was working, we will not know until we all meet her in heaven. The shock was a terrible one to all of us, coming as it did on the top of the terrible persecutions, and the fiercest financial test the work has ever had. I do not like to emphasize the opinion expressed by some that poison was brought into our home by our enemies.

My wife had not been enjoying good health for some time, and all felt that she should have a change and take a furlough in the homeland. For this, kind friends from Pastor Offler's church in Seattle had cabled the fare for my wife and our family. The journey could have been made some weeks previous to the death of Mary Anna but the Lord checked us from allowing the trip, and all we could do was wait. The day following the death of Mary Anna, the burden was lifted, and we all felt free in the spirit for the furlough to be undertaken.

Perhaps one of the most difficult things in my life was to meet our dear children the morning following the death of Mary Anna to tell them that she had gone to heaven. During our fight of faith for her life, dear Sister Stromquist had taken the children to another room, and it was wonderful to hear them hang on to the throne of God for Mary Anna. The next morning I had to gather them around my knees and tell them that she was in heaven. Of course they all broke down, and I, too, but God was sufficient, and my fears that the children's faith would be shaken were all unnecessary.

God had graciously given victory as I watched the passing away of Mary Anna in my arms at midnight, but the next day such terrible fears and reasonings came from the evil one. I was literally battling with demons for hours at a time. Circumstances were such that I was unable to ask outsiders to conduct the funeral service, but praise the Lord I was able to rejoice in Him and give Him the glory during the funeral as I stood with the coffin of Mary Anna at my side. As always His grace was sufficient and He was a wonderful hiding place in this time of storm.

152 IMPOSSIBILITIES BECOME CHALLENGES

My wife and three children left for Seattle, my wife's birthplace, staying there for a period of recuperation and rebuilding up of her body. Although she was an American citizen by birth, the rules applying to aliens prohibiting them from staying in the States over a period of twelve months equally applied to her and the children as she had lost her U.S.A. citizenship by marriage, so I was facing stern problems as to the placing of my family after that time elapsed.

As we prayed over matters and realized that my wife's health and strength had not returned as quickly as expected, it was considered to be the will of the Lord that she visit my people in England who had never met her or our family.

This was a problem indeed. It meant transporting my wife and three children across the whole of the American continent, the Atlantic Ocean, as well as providing for them during their stay in England, and the return journey, besides the support of the work in Japan. As we chatted with several friends about these matters, we were made to understand that these were absolutely impossibilities in these times of depression and financial uneasiness. We, too, realized that these things represented questions of a larger magnitude than we had previously tackled, but at the same time felt a secret assurance that God was teaching us more and more to believe Him for the solution of greater and more complex problems.

Brother H. B. Taylor of San Antonio, Texas, had given me an invitation to hold an evangelistic campaign some time with him, and correspondence revealed that he wished me to come over during the summer months of 1931 to hold this campaign. On the way I was able to spend a few days with my family in Seattle. It was a daring step of faith for, though Sister Dithridge from Tachikawa had graciously offered to give me special help during my absence, I had to return to Japan within four months at the very latest.

Until the very last minute it was a debatable question as to whether I should go or not. Inwardly, I was fully assured

PROBLEMS MET AND OVERCOME 153

of the will of the Lord, but the way financially had not yet been opened. All the missions, workers, and Bible School students had to be supported in my absence, and so I had to move in God, first to receive His assurance of being in His divine will, and then to receive a manifestation of what I felt to be His will.

I was finally able to book my passage on a Japanese steamer, third class, eating Japanese food. While staying with my wife and children a few days in Seattle, faith was given to trust God for the fares of my family across the American Continent, then across the Atlantic Ocean to England to stay with my people for a period of time.

It may be amusing to some to know that I took with me to San Antonio my eldest daughter Faith (later she became Mrs. Wally Denton) buying her ticket right through to New York, leaving my other two children and my wife in Seattle to follow as the Lord opened the way. After my campaign was half over, my wife and family were able to join me in San Antonio due to the generosity of Brother Taylor and the saints in San Antonio. The last week of the campaign was drawing to a close. No mention was made of the need for the purchasing of tickets for my wife and family from New York to Liverpool. Many possibly thought that these tickets were all bought, but day after day definite "looks" toward heaven were being made, trusting in God's good providences, that He would honor the faith exercised and enable the family to journey towards New York, as I turned my face again toward Seattle and the Orient.

The day before I had to pay over the cash for the Atlantic passages for my family, God placed in my hand the exact amount sufficient for the fares, and again the joy bells were ringing as God so graciously manifested His love and power toward us.

Various were the tests, and gracious were the answers to prayer granted by the Lord to my wife during her stay in England. I endeavored to send enough from what God sent me in Japan to supply her needs during her stay there. I was not always able to send to her at the same time of the

IMPOSSIBILITIES BECOME CHALLENGES

month, or the same amount, so that my wife had to look to God constantly for supplies. On more than one occasion the last penny was spent when, by the very next mail, a letter from Japan, registered, would bring funds for more supplies. Thus it was proved over and over again that no circumstances nor times are too difficult nor too complex for God to supply daily needs for those who dare to trust Him fully.

And now the time (one year later) had come for the return of the family to Japan. God had graciously given to us another little girlie, Grace. The witness that the family should return to Japan was received at both ends of the line. The amount required for the fares from England to Japan, across the whole of the American Continent and across two oceans, for a family of six, amounted to nothing less than $1,000, or two hundred pounds. "Is anything too hard for the Lord?"

As the matter was thought over and brought before the throne of God, it was made clear that it was not right to expect my wife to make this long tedious journey, with a new baby, alone. But for myself to again leave the shores of Japan was only to make myself a mark for tremendous criticisms on the part of many in the homeland who might not know the inner workings, and the circumstances, surrounding the visits.

As on the previous visit to the homelands, I still refused all offerings being taken in meetings at which I spoke, trusting God entirely for every penny required for traveling fares and for the expenses on route, besides the large commitments for the work in Japan. Some may think that we had a reserve account in Japan which we left for the work's support during our absence. This was not the case. We had left the work in Japan for visits to the homelands three times up to the year 1932, and each time the treasury had been practically empty. We are more convinced that the greatest thing in life is to know assuredly the will of the Lord, and then go ahead in obedience to His will.

The missionaries working in full fellowship have each

PROBLEMS MET AND OVERCOME 155

time very graciously exercised the same faith as ourselves, and have at great cost and sacrifice to themselves undertaken the executive side of the work, for which we know that God will grant His own reward to them.

Again Sister Dithridge felt it was the will of the Lord to come to help in the Bible School permitting me to leave Japan to bring my family back from England. But what a task I had ahead of me if I did this! I had first to receive my own fare from Japan to England, practically half way around the world. Then after arriving in England I had to receive from the Lord the fare back again to Japan for myself and for the rest of the family.

Everywhere people were talking depression. In mission after mission there were hardly any who had regular work. Hundreds and thousands of God's people were on relief and had nothing wherewith to help even the local work. But praise the Lord, God is greater than any situation, and He is able to supply more than is necessary for the fulfillment of His will.

Once having received the assurance that it was His will to go to England for the family, I knew the only thing to do was to go, and though friends and foes alike might criticize and talk, all I had to do was to go right ahead, and God would Himself open doors that no man could close. Hallelujah!

Not being connected officially with any of the branches of the Full Gospel movement in England rather hindered my visit there, but God helped me. The same attitude regarding my meetings for my own expenses or work was upheld though I granted the taking of offerings for other "work", according to the desire of the local assembly or pastor.

"When he putteth forth his own sheep, he goeth before them, and the sheep follow him: for they know his voice." Praise the Lord! Within a period of about four months we were able to book through tickets from Liverpool, England, to Kobe, Japan. We took our leave of friends and relatives again giving glory to God who had so miraculously undertaken for us, without our mentioning our needs to man.

This was victory indeed. Arriving in England without any funds I found my wife and family in the same condition. I was financially responsible for the work in Japan, and in the very shortest possible time it was absolutely necessary that I obtain the full fares for the trip back to Japan for the six of us, across two oceans, Atlantic and Pacific, as well as across the whole length of the American Continent.

True, we had our difficulties. After arranging with the steamship company for the amount of the tickets and the steamer, the steamship company turned at the last minute and charged us with a higher rate of exchange than we had first agreed upon. This point almost capsized our financial boat. We had hardly gotten over this difficulty when we were informed that our eldest daughter would be charged full fare because she had just passed her eleventh birthday. This was another smack from the enemy to move us from our God-given position.

In one case, the Lord told one of His stewards to give me a certain amount for the return fare "if I called to see her." There was no possibility of my doing this in the natural. She lived in a town where I did not speak, and which I would never visit in the ordinary course of events. Of course, I knew nothing of the Word of God to her, but in a strange way it came to me to go and see her. I was surprised myself at the leading, and more surprised when I heard from her own lips what God had bade her do but, praising the Lord again for His wonderful ways, this incident proved of fresh inspiration to believe day by day that our lives are in His hands, and He does care for us.

This is the story. My wife had saved what local letters she had received for me to peruse through upon my arrival in order that I might be guided in any visits I made to missions in England. Among others, there was a very short and simple letter from a lady sending my wife baby clothes for our latest arrival, Grace Lydia. Surely there was nothing special in such a letter, and yet as I read it I was compelled to place that particular letter at one side and reread the

PROBLEMS MET AND OVERCOME 157

same again. Why or how I cannot explain, but there was something about that ordinary, very simple note about the forwarding of the clothes that caught the attention of my soul, and for two or three days I prayed over it. As I did so, I was compelled to believe that God had some purpose in this beyond my natural understanding. Following this leading and conviction, I felt there would be no harm done to write a short note saying how I felt, which I did, even saying that if it were the will of the Lord, I might even go and see her. Of course, the devil teased me by saying, "Fancy, writing a lady in another town that you feel led to go and see her to thank her for sending baby clothes. Why, you are crazy."

It pays to obey the Lord no matter how foolish it seems or how the devil may tease. A simple reply came saying that it would be all right to make the visit. I continued to pray, determined to only go as directed by the Lord, for I was not going to pay out the railway fare unless I was absolutely certain that this was in the will of the Lord. I picture myself now arriving about lunch time and having a bite to eat at a local restaurant. After finding the house, I walked up and down in front of it praying and determining to return unless I had an absolute assurance that I was in the fullest will of the Lord in coming. Praise God I had it, and at the time appointed knocked on the door. What was I going to say? And for what reason had I come? Honestly, I can say, I did not know the answer. If I judge things from the natural point of view, I had never taken a more foolish stand. But I was dealing with an Omnipotent and Omniscient God. Hallelujah.

I admit after I had made myself known, I felt just a little embarrassed. In fact I told the dear lady so. "Oh, no," she replied, "there is no need to feel that way. I know why you have come. There is not the slightest need to say a word. You have just obeyed the Lord." With these words she left the room. In a moment she returned with a check already written out for 50 pounds, saying that the Lord had told her to give me this amount towards the return fare of the family, "if Mr. Coote comes to see me without being asked to

158 IMPOSSIBILITIES BECOME CHALLENGES

come." I left praising the Lord for another proof that our God is a living, eternal and mighty God, according to the Bible.

Even when the gangplanks had been pulled up for the departure of the boat from Liverpool for New York, God again undertook. We wondered why the boat did not leave on the scheduled time. But the London boat train was late, and I believe God permitted this train to be late to meet our needs. Just as the bustling was going on at the arrival of the train, a lady hurriedly came to the pier with a note for myself. The note contained help for our journey which, had we not received, we would have been short of funds.

Praise the Lord, too, for the wonderful way He undertook on the New York pier. We had been given to understand that our baggage would be cared for by the steamship company and bonded through to Japan without any additional expense.

We had made no provision for handling our baggage at New York, and our sole possession was a $10 bill to pay for the storage of a trunk that we had left at New York on the previous trip. The time for closing the customs shed was overdue. The baggage man was a little vexed as he called out rather roughly, "$15.00 it will cost you!" and put out his hand for money. I did not have the money but God is never late to supply. Hallelujah! Mrs. Norris had met the boat, and though we had not let anyone know our address in New York, a friend had felt distinctly led to hand to her a few dollars for us. She gave it to us in an envelope, so after hearing the demand for $15.00, we walked down the pier crying, "Lord, help us now." We were told to look into the envelope, which we did, and found the money. We paid the baggage man and rejoiced again at the wonderful dealings of our God.

My wife had not made sufficient allowance of milk for the baby. She told me that evening that we would need milk for the morning. How we were to buy it I did not know. The devil kept me awake all night listening to his reasoning that the child would cry for hunger, and that folks would find out our condition and that I would lose my faith, and that would be the end of matters. The devil is certainly a liar.

I had told no one our New York address for we had only intended staying there a night or two. However, the next morning just as we were eating breakfast we received a "Special Delivery" letter containing financial help sufficient to buy the baby's milk. We were so full of gratitude and praise to God that we could not keep the matter to ourselves. As we testified to what God had done, another brother broke right down, confessing that the Lord had told him the night before to give us $5.00, and that he had disobeyed the Lord. With tears he made his confession.

This was the story of God's dealings again from New York, across the whole continent to Seattle. Two of the children were taken down with mumps. Throughout one night we battled with death in the city of Winnipeg and it seemed at any moment we would lose our little Grace. But God was merciful to us.

The last attempt of the enemy to prevent our returning was in Seattle the night before sailing. We had been driven by car quite a long distance to preach. On the return journey, away from the post office, telegraph office or human habitation, the car broke down, and for a while refused to move. All possibilities of arriving in time for the boat seemed to go. But God, and prayer. We arrived home at four in the morning, packed and left the shores of America again for dear old Japan.

CHAPTER TWENTY

BIBLE SCHOOL'S FIRST GRADUATION

*"And the things that thou hast heard of me among many
witnesses, the same commit thou to faithful men,
who shall be able to teach others also."
(2 Timothy 2:2)*

March 1933 was a happy time for after years of strugling, we finally saw eight of the Bible School students finish their training and go out into fulltime ministry.

Not only had there been opposition from the ungodly, but even from Christian circles. Some felt it was not scriptural to have a Bible School, and in measure, we also oppose the dead, formal, highly critical "cemeteries" which theological seminaries are so often prone to be.

In the history of the Ikoma Bible School up until today, it has been anything but a cemetery. During the first few months of operation, many more than the first eight who graduated were accepted, but either the high standard of life or the vigorous demands proved too much for many and they turned to other professions. This is because the Bible School was not to just train the head, but our principal aim has been the training of the heart to give their whole lives to the preaching of the gospel.

Others have opposed the school on the basis that the church should be the place where ministers receive their training. Again I fully agree with the principle but believe it must be adapted to the varying circumstances found existing on foreign fields.

The conditions in Japan under which both men and women work are such that ordinary converts have little opportunity to attend spiritual meetings in the assembly. I have often heard the heart cryings of new converts who yearn for more spiritual food who have to work long hours, not getting home until nine or ten at night.

BIBLE SCHOOL'S FIRST GRADUATION 161

It was obvious, therefore, that if we were to fulfill our call "Japan and Pentecost until Jesus comes," some means of training the nationals was necessary. It must be noted that though a new convert may immediately enter into total forgiveness of sin and feel God's power in his soul, usually he has absolutely no knowledge whatsoever regarding biblical principles.

Often during our tent campaigns in the summer we have been asked the difference between the Bible and the song book. "Is the song book inspired like the Bible?" "If not, why is the Bible alone inspired?"

It is not necessary to defend the existence of the Bible School. Anyone who has read the remarkable way God led toward its building cannot help but feel the divine touch about it. While we were compelled to give it the name "Ikoma Bible School" to comply with the laws in Japan, it is in fact merely an assembly where men and women who are called of God may be free to read the Word, hear it expounded, help in evangelistic work, and gain practical experience in spiritual matters. Following this, they are thrust out by the Spirit into areas where there will be absolutely no Christian fellowship to draw from.

Our plan is that the Bible School shall eventually become self-supporting. Every student now gives four hours of his time to manual labor, either helping produce vegetables, or working in the printing department, printing special magazines and tracts, or in the building department, erecting churches for God's glory.

Soon after the graduation of the first eight students, the Japan Pentecostal Church was formed as an organization to cover the churches that were being formed.

Our vision is a self-supporting, self-governing and self-propagating church for Japan, and to this end, each Bible School student was taught to work.

As I review the events of the Bible School during its first thirty years, I am amazed at what has taken place: hundreds brought under mighty conviction, tremendous confessions made, hungerings for the fullness of the Spirit and the

IMPOSSIBILITIES BECOME CHALLENGES

mighty outpourings of the Holy Ghost!

I remember a splendid young Baptist student who came. He had a slight deformity in one of his legs which prevented him from entering a college of his own denomination. As he listened to the Word day after day, he became interested in the Holy Spirit, Pentecostal fashion. At times he appeared opposed to our emphasis on a personal Pentecost, but what a joy one Monday to hear a thud right over my office, after I had listened to his earnest praying and praising God! Soon after the thud, he fell under the mighty power of God and began to speak with other tongues, glorifying the Lord!

It was this fellow who spent his summer riding a bicycle throughout Japan searching out his relatives and ministering to them the baptism of the Holy Ghost. He was instrumental in bringing over thirty of them into the Pentecostal experience.

The Ikoma Bible College was not limited to Japanese. Many Koreans came to the school and proved to be wonderful students. A Manchurian studied with us for a time, and later two of our Formosan graduates returned to Formosa with a burning desire to see a Pentecostal outpouring in their country. As they thanked me for what the school had done for them, they asked, "Will you please make an appeal for Pentecostal work in our homeland, Formosa?"

I wish that those who were not in favor of the Bible College could have been with us at the 1954 New Year's convention when our seven young ladies from Okinawa broke down and wept as if their hearts would break, as they pled with God for a visitation of His Spirit upon Okinawa. I promised them that in God's time I would definitely seek to go there and help bring a moving of the Spirit upon Okinawa.

CHAPTER TWENTY ONE

SMALL CHURCHES

"He loveth our nation, and he hath
built us a synagogue."
(Luke 7:5)

One of the greatest difficulties in fulfilling our God given call "Japan and Pentecost" has been the high prices asked for renting buildings. Adding to this problem were the crowded conditions everywhere and the small size of most available buildings.

The population in Japan has increased with such rapidity and being an island empire without means for expansion, houses and shops are much smaller than those found in western lands.

If we rented a tiny house to use as a mission, our evangelism would be dwarfed. If, on the other hand, a larger place were secured, the prospects of the church becoming self-supporting in a short time became remote.

Despite the above problems, we are distinctly assured that the will of God is for this message of the full gospel to be preached to every Japanese in this generation!

It is said: "Where there is a will, there is a way," and I believe this same principle holds true in spiritual work, that is, provided the conviction comes directly from heaven. Difficulties may arise and the matter appear to be impossible but God, by His Spirit, Who has given the conviction, will likewise reveal a way for its fulfillment.

In the summer of 1931, while I was in America, three of our students with a burden to preach the gospel in the town of Nukata spent their summer holiday there. Prior to this, they had held roadside Sunday Schools for the children, but now God burdened them for the spiritual needs of the people. A few inquirers were seeking God which greatly encouraged them in their efforts.

IMPOSSIBILITIES BECOME CHALLENGES

During this period of living by faith, one of these students received a vision of building a tiny "Barrack Church." This he did and for an outlay of about Yen 400.00 ($200.00 on the then ruling exchange) he was able to build a building holding about 80 people.

The building was not finished with plastered walls and other decorations, but was sufficient for holding meetings. The question was raised whether the authorities would grant the permit for this as a church, but our fears were dispelled soon after when the permit came. Thus the Lord began to show me that here was one solution to the tantalizing problem of many years as to how we could fulfill our command to go into every area of Japan with the Pentecostal message.

We had tent meetings in various prefectures, and also witnessed scores of Japanese in various out of the way places receiving the Holy Ghost, but their knowledge of the Word was so scant. Much teaching and pastoring must be done to conserve the results.

The family system in Japan is such that young people are to obey not only parents but other members of the larger family circle and consult with them regarding points of religion. To go against the opinions and decisions of the family circle is one of the worst crimes that a Japanese can commit. Thus a definite place for meeting and a place to pastor those brought under the spell of the gospel was vital.

The vision of building a small church helps in this situation. Where God's Spirit is poured out, and funds so permit, it is contemplated that one of these buildings be erected for the caring of the converts. This could be done at that time for $1,000. However, since then costs have risen so high, it now takes $5,000 for a small building. This small building will gather about 100 people together and they will have a place where they feel free to worship God according to the Word. They will also have an opportunity to testify to others and, by their small offerings, the sundry expenses of the building, lights, ground rent and other incidentals, will be met by the converts themselves.

SMALL CHURCHES

Praise God a number of small buildings are already erected, and others are now on the way. We are believing that God will give us the faith and courage to build many more during the following years. The time occupied in building is about three months, the Bible School students doing some of the work, when the location permits.

While we call these buildings small churches, it must be remembered that they are fully equipped buildings but minus the extra decorations that go to make a building look nice. These matters will be attended to later by the Christians themselves as they are able to help with their offerings.

We believe this is a distinct and novel plan for men and women in the homeland who feel they would like to have a permanent part in saving souls from atheism. Since the Pacific War, prices of materials have greatly increased. While we were able to build these Barrack Churches before the war for $1,000, we now find it takes considerable more. Speaking as of 1954, our faith is to be able to build small churches in other areas surrounding Osaka and Kyoto.

IKOMA CHURCH

CHAPTER TWENTY TWO

ON TO KOREA

*"And this gospel of the kingdom shall be preached
in all the world for a witness unto all nations;
and then shall the end come."*
(Matthew 24:14)

Though the land of Korea had a wonderful touch from
God and a real revival several years ago, it is surprising that
she became one of the last nations to receive the Pentecostal blessing. I have often wondered why it is that the Full
Gospel people neglected this nation, thinking possibly that
because of the revival she enjoyed soon after the Welsch
revival that she did not need the fuller blessing of the Holy
Ghost.

But God is not unmindful of His promise to pour out of
His Spirit upon all flesh, and many Koreans residing in
Japan before the war were filled with the Holy Spirit,
speaking with other tongues as on the day of Pentecost.

Since the Pacific War various missionaries have gone to
Korea and what has rejoiced our hearts perhaps as much as
anything is to receive letters from former Korean graduates
of Ikoma Bible College telling us that they have pioneered
for the Pentecostal truth and are now pastoring small
churches. Six of these pastors at the time of writing this
revised issue of the book are pleading for me to visit Korea
and I have just received permission from the United Nations to visit these places during the summer of 1954, and
am trusting God to direct my thoughts and efforts in this
land.

Before the war on account of the large number of
Koreans residing in the city of Osaka one of our churches in
that city became Korean. It later became self-supporting,
and the believers themselves built their own church.
However, on account of the confusion at the end of the war,
and also the trouble with the Communists and the North

ON TO KOREA 167

Koreans, this building has not yet been returned to the believers at the time of this writing.

I am assured that God's calling is without repentance. In the original book "Twenty Years in Japan," I wrote the following passage:

"We believe it is God's will that a Bible Training School be erected in Korea itself for the training of Koreans to be their own pastors and evangelists. God is wonderfully preparing workers for the school. He will provide the funds and we shall have workers already trained and equipped to become teachers and helpers in this forward move in Korea."

At the beginning of the year 1936, I was brought under a heavy spiritual cloud. This lasted for almost a month, but on January 21st I received the following letter from America:

Dear Brother Coote:

I thank God for being able to enclose a check for $3,300 for the work you are doing for Him. This is in the nature of an investment as I was not happy concerning its former use. I should suggest the following ways of using it:

Work in Korea	$1,000.00
Tent Campaign Work	1,000.00
A Small Church	500.00
Bible School Wing or	
Support of Students	500.00
	$3,000.00

As regarding the $300, I do not know what loss may be incurred over exchange, so leave it for that or any need of yours. I do not wish my name to appear in the matter. God bless you all especially with the blessing of Isaiah 40:29-31.

Your sister in Jesus Christ

Upon reading this letter the above mentioned cloud

168 IMPOSSIBILITIES BECOME CHALLENGES

disappeared forever. I took the letter over to my wife to read and, after thinking a moment, she said, "Leonard, do you know what today is?" I had not thought anything about the day or the date. Immediately my wife spoke up saying, "Today is the anniversary of Mary Anna's death." And in the same way as the Lord sent in the first $1,000 toward the purchase of the ground for the Japan work (on the first anniversary of the great Japanese earthquake), so the Lord sent in the first $1,000 for the start of the Korean work in Korea on the anniversary of the passing of our daughter, Mary Anna.

"Just a coincidence," some might say. To which I answer, there have been too many of them to be mere coincidences. First, the first offering coming on the very first day of my stepping out on God's Word as a missionary; then the coming of the first offering to purchase the ground for the Japan headquarters on the very anniversary of the great earthquake, and now the coming of this offering earmarked for Korea, on the very day, not a day earlier, nor a day later, but on the very day that Mary Anna was taken from us. Surely, if these things are called coincidences, they are Godly ones, arranged by the hand that created this wonderful world of ours!

Was it a coincidence that Christ was born in Bethlehem when the Old Testament tells us He was going to be born there? Was it a coincidence that Christ was born of the virgin Mary, when Isaiah predicted: "The Lord Himself shall give you a sign: Behold a virgin shall conceive and bear a son, and shall call His name Immanuel?"

Here was a definite confirmation that we were now to consider extending our borders to Korea. Our call was: "Japan and Pentecost until Jesus comes." At first our narrow thinking limited us to preaching in a couple of missions in one city. The Japanese earthquake awakened us to the fact that Japan was not confined to one city. Now, even through the sudden death of our fourth child, God was including Korea in our vision. At that time, Korea was occupied by Japan, and was part of Japan.

ON TO KOREA

It would make too large a book to go into all the difficulties and tremendous answers to prayer regarding purchasing the land for the headquarters of the Korean work and the necessary steps for the work to be started there.

After many preliminary preparations, Pastors Kaku (Korean), Yamamoto (Japanese) and I (British), spent one week in the capital to purchase the ground there. From early morning to late at night scores of plots of land were investigated in every section of the city. Much prayer had been made that God would guide us with His eye. Experience gained in choosing the headquarters site for the Japan field enabled us to meet each obstacle and fight the fight of faith to a successful end.

Finally the revelation as to the right location came. Praise God for the wonderful revelations of His divine will. Though we three agreed on the location, the price was prohibitive, and the owner refused to sell to us. Had we been mistaken? Conviction grew that we were being led of the Lord, and still the opposition was as stiff as ever. A holiness pastor endeavored to act as a go between for us, but the owner was adamant, refusing to have any more interviews with us. Hope receded and it seemed like we would have to give up and try some other location. Suddenly light dawned in my soul. I heard that the owner had been to America, that he spoke English well, and that his wife was an earnest Christian. "I'll go see him myself," I said, for this thought had come to me direct from heaven. I presented myself, and though he treated me roughly at first, he finally softened.

"You want the land for a Bible School?" he asked, "Can you assure me that is perfectly true? Where is your proof?" I was not ready to answer such questions or give such proofs, but like a flash I looked into my satchel where I had a copy of our magazine "Japan and Pentecost" giving a two page article about God's challenge regarding our building a Bible School in Korea. He read it, and his attitude changed completely. He sold us the land at close to our own price, arranged the transfer, and helped the deal go through

170   IMPOSSIBILITIES BECOME CHALLENGES

smoothly. Why? Because it was the Lord's will.

At first there were several complications as Japan had become an independent nation and the conflict between the Communistic North Korea and the Free South Korea made things difficult. But my attitude was "Give me this mountain." Having received the permit from the United Nations for an exploratory visit to Korea, I accepted the invitation of six of our former students to preach in their churches. I went to Korea trusting God to open the way for the clearance of all difficulties concerning the property and to move on the hearts of His people in the homeland for the building of the Korean Bible Training School.

The following two paragraphs were in our former book "Twenty Five Years in Japan":

"At the time of writing (June 1939) no buildings have yet been erected, although it had been hoped that there would be this year. Yen 2,500 is in hand, and movements are on foot for the necessary permits to be received right away.

"Singularly, in much the same way that God marvelously confirmed His will in the location of the Ikoma Bible Campus, we have recently heard that soon after the purchase of the Korean school ground, on account of the China hostilities, all Europeans have been prevented from purchasing ground in that peninsula. Surely God again has wonderfully guided as to the time of making this purchase for His work there."

CHAPTER TWENTY THREE

JAPAN'S BIBLE SCHOOL, SECOND WING

"Speak unto the Children of Israel, that they go forward."
(Exodus 14:15)

Some of our friends were surprised when they heard that I was considering enlarging the capacity of the Bible School by building another wing the same size as the first wing, but with three stories. The Bible School had become the headquarters for the evangelistic activities of the Japan Apostolic Mission, as well as for the various churches that had been formed in different prefectures. Various conventions are held at different times of the year, including Sunday School rallies, and the chapel in the first wing of the school being crowded out it was felt a special convention hall should be built or another wing added.

In addition to the first wing that is recorded in the earlier chapters of this book, a women's dormitory had been erected where women students stayed. There was also an annex which housed the matron's family, with rooms for visitors, plus an extra dining room and large kitchen. This annex now provides living quarters for Bible School students.

Much prayer was given to the matter, and before we made any decisions we had many conferences with the contractors. Having the witness that this was of God, and receiving permission from the authorities, the excavation for the full basement began. For a couple of years this basement with a temporary roof, served as our convention hall, but when the rainy season came the following year, the Lord said: "Arise and build!"

Things were different from the building of the first wing. Then we had the money in hand, but this time God commanded us to give the contract and go ahead by faith. For several reasons, it was necessary for the work to be finished by a set time. This demanded extreme care to avoid any

172 IMPOSSIBILITIES BECOME CHALLENGES

mistake with the contract. The amount of money involved was far greater than for the first wing. When the day came for me to sign the contract instead of feeling heavy in my spirit because of the immensity of the work, I felt as light as a feather. I had committed myself to thousands of dollars which I did not possess. The payments had to be made on determined dates, and yet I had no idea where the money would come from.

Praise God for a wonderful confirmation! The contract was signed at four in the afternoon and without knowing this, a European lady asked to have a word with me at eight o'clock that night. "I have prayed about this and am assured I have the will of the Lord. Please accept the enclosed funds for the work of the Lord under your care" were the words given with a substantial sum for His cause.

Praise God, He makes no mistakes. I admit we had many difficulties. The building program occupied a hectic three months. It was summer and my family was away in the hills trying to escape the great heat. Many times conferences between the contractor, my secretary and myself lasted until eight or nine o'clock at night. Frequently, exhausted from the day's work, I would forget to buy food, and by then, it would be too late. But what a joy to be hard at it in the service of the King! It was even a joy on more than one occasion to get a bite of dry, hard bread bordering on mold to appease my hunger before bed time. Not that there was not money for food, but the work had so occupied time and thought, food had been forgotten.

Today the second wing of the Japan Bible School stands out majestically as proof that God answers prayer and honors faith. Here they are, twelve buildings on the compound comprising of:

Bible School - first wing, annex and second wing with
    full basement.

Executive office - a three story building

Missionary Home - with my small apartment attached
    (in all, eight bed rooms)

Missionaries' homes - three separate houses

JAPAN'S BIBLE SCHOOL, SECOND WING

Native Teachers' homes - three separate houses
Printing Plant - store and work rooms

The above are all fully paid for, without any debt or mortgage, besides eight other church buildings in various prefectures.

SECOND WING OF BIBLE COLLEGE

CHAPTER TWENTY FOUR

VISIT TO AUSTRALIA AND NEW ZEALAND

*"At the commandment of the Lord they rested in the
tents, and at the commandment of the Lord they
journeyed, they kept the charge of the Lord,
at the commandment of the Lord
by the hand of Moses."
(Numbers 9:23)*

For some time I had an inward witness that the Lord would have me visit Australia to present the work in Japan. It was no surprise to me therefore, when an invitation to do so under the auspices of the Apostolic Church came from Pastor Gardner, chairman of the Missionary Board.

A considerable time was spent in prayer before giving my reply, and due to the great distance between Australia and Japan, and the inconvenient steamer service, I knew that my timing was of the utmost importance.

When assured of God's will in this, my wife loyally agreed to look after the office for six months during my absence. But in order for her to do this, I needed to provide help for the teaching of our children. At first, this seemed an insurmountable obstacle, as we had tried many times before to get help in this area to no avail. But the Lord arranged that a single lady who was visiting Japan as a tourist advertised in the paper, wanting employment so she could stay longer. Arrangements were made for her to teach our children, and farewells were said.

After a long dreary journey across the equator, Brisbane was reached which was my first appointment. The Apostolic Church had arranged a splendid itinerary for me. Just prior to my first service I had to smile, as I was interviewed by Pastor Cathcart saying certain rumors had surfaced regarding a supposed belief that I denied the personality of the Holy Spirit. Again I was made aware of how real the dealings of the Lord had been, and yet at the

VISIT TO AUSTRALIA AND NEW ZEALAND 175

same time, how definitely the oppositions of the enemy come to discourage! The Lord had beautifully led to make this visit to Australia, and yet here was the devil, trying to hinder and spoil God's purposes. But praise the Lord, he is not only a liar, but a defeated foe! Praise the name of the Lord!

Splendid meetings were held throughout the Commonwealth, especially at Brisbane, Sydney, Melbourne, Adelaide and Perth. God graciously gave liberty at many of these places, resulting in the coming to Japan of Miss Olive Hughes from Perth to be my secretary, and Miss Leta Dunn from New Zealand to teach our children. We had often wondered why God had not answered our prayers regarding a secretary and teacher for our children, but "God moves in mysterious ways His wonders to perform; He plants His feet upon the waves and rides upon the storm." Now, after many years, these prayers were answered. Miss Hughes had been seeking for years an opportunity to come to Japan for missionary work, and now her call was being fulfilled. Miss Dunn had received a definite call to give herself for the education of missionary children in Japan, and being a retired school teacher, her spiritual goal was now about to be fulfilled. What a gracious God we serve!

Five other missionaries came to Japan as a result of my visit to Australia, including Wally Denton who later married our daughter Faith, and, who, several years later founded Life Temple in Dallas, Texas.

God graciously undertook in many ways during this visit to Australia, and also in the hurried trip through New Zealand. Before agreeing to go to Australia, I had stipulated my desire to the leaders that though missionary offerings could be taken for the Apostolic Church fund, I felt I was to come without any salary or financial remuneration, that I should look to the Lord for the support of the work in Japan and my own personal needs. As the result of this stand of faith, the Lord raised up new friends and prayer support for the work in Japan.

CHAPTER TWENTY FIVE

THE PACIFIC WAR

"And we know that all things work together for good to them that love God, to them who are the called according to his purpose."
(Romans 8:28)

It will seem incongruous to some to place Romans 8:28 at the top of this chapter dealing with the horrible Pacific War (World War II), when so many of England and America's finest young men were destroyed. Yet, as I look back to the events preceding Pearl Harbor I must bow my head and heart again in recognition that there is a God in heaven and His eye is on His children, and He causes conditions to happen and strange things to protect those who are the apple of his eye.

Though conditions were serious, and persecution sternly felt before the outbreak of the war, our hearts were still aflame with the need of evangelizing the Japanese. As soon as the winter's severe cold passed, we were on our knees asking God for the right location for the spring tent campaigns. One of our workers was assigned to go into likely cities to locate suitable sites for the tent and make proper arrangements with the governing officials.

These tent campaigns were mighty efforts to capture cities for God. The usual procedure was to choose a city of 30,000 to 50,000 people and begin to focus on that city with much prayer, and concentrate every effort there. The wheels of the printing press would move faster as thousands of handbills, tracts, and literature were prepared for a house to house visitation with help from the Bible School students.

I always tried to accompany the first trucks carrying the tent equipment and seats so I could imbibe the nature of the city to which I was to bring the gospel. The Japanese are an inquisitive people, and it was always amusing to listen to their conversations as they gathered around while the trucks

THE PACIFIC WAR 177

were being unloaded and the tent put up. "I wonder what it is?" one would say. Others would reply, "It may be an open air movie show." Then when they saw me, some would say, "Douglas Fairbanks has come to town!" Not that I look like Douglas Fairbanks by any means, but that as the American pictures have often been shown in this city, where no Europeans resided, they mistook me for any movie idol they had ever seen.

And for the next month it would be a fight of faith; a real onslaught against the powers of heathenism as we invaded the strongholds of the enemy. We usually would find two or three old houses which we rented temporarily, and without furniture, using boxes and making shift the best we could, we settled in for a real battle for souls. Each morning after breakfast we gathered for worship and prayer. We then divided into four or five groups to cover the city with our hands filled with gospels and tracts to visit every house. We had trained the Bible School students to try to get into the houses, pray with the occupants and lead them to Christ even before the first message had been given in the tent.

A compulsory time of rest preceded the afternoon prayer meeting which was followed by a series of street meetings, usually three or four to an afternoon, held in a different section of the city each day. While my wife conducted the evening children's service in the tent, I would be on my face laying hold of the horns of the altar for the night service.

The children's meetings were tremendous! Oh, that you could attend one of them! It was exciting to see up to one thousand eager faces of these children who do not know what Sunday School is, who have never heard about Jesus Christ, listen with rapt attention to the Bible story, and many of them made almost instant decisions to receive the Lord.

It was never difficult to gather the children, but our problem was how to get rid of them after their service, so they would not hinder the adult service that night. God gave us wisdom to handle this by having a children's street

178 IMPOSSIBILITIES BECOME CHALLENGES

march around the city with lighted lanterns, and having the children sing with a loud voice to help us invite their parents to the next service, and this so thoroughly wore them out, they were glad to retire to their homes for rest, enabling us to have the adult service undisturbed.

But these pioneer efforts were always conducted in the midst of severe persecution, both from the authorities and the public. Some times we had to do a lot of explaining to the police about our motives, and at times they demanded that a policeman sit on the platform. Other times they demanded every message be written out before being delivered so they could inspect the content. We felt hemmed in.

Often, a very officious person would come up to me at the beginning of a service saying he must see me immediately. Usually his first word was: "What right have you to hold this service?" or "Who gave you permission to hold this campaign?" Usually this person would prove to be some upstart who was very antichristian in attitude.

On two or three occasions a policeman came to the Bible School and even while I was teaching demanded I accompany him to the police station. He did not let me end the class, but insisted I leave with him at once. At the police station they would quiz me on and on over some trivial point. On each of these occasions it became clear that there was no issue involved, but it was an effort to get me ruffled. It became evident that some times they were after bribes, and that they were trying to discourage our pioneer evangelism efforts.

As World War II drew near, the political conditions worsened and it became more and more difficult to obtain permits for special meetings. The police were becoming more and more troublesome. It seemed like they were in our offices every day. In the morning two or three would come together, asking many questions, then sit around smoking, and we could do nothing about it. When they left, before you had time to take your breath, three or four more would come and ask the same questions. They would not

THE PACIFIC WAR   179

be satisfied with the statement we had already given, and we had to go through this again and again, while they took their time and filled our offices with their smoke.

Though I did not expect the Japanese to do what they did at Pearl Harbor, it was becoming evident that things were worsening. But an omniscient God knows the end from the beginning, and He saw the conflict coming. Thank God we were in His hands, and He manipulated things so we would be secure from the cruel ways of these people in time of war. The daughter of one of our most faithful workers was taken down with galloping tuberculosis, and our second daughter Ruth was her best friend. The two girls spent many hours together, our Ruth often spending the night while the girl's father was away in tent meetings helping me.

It is dreadful to watch the terrible nature of galloping consumption. In a very short time the progress of this disease turned this lovely charming girl into nothing but skin and bones, and she could not be recognized as the former, active, smiling, beautiful daughter of our worker.

Because of the terrible nature of the sickness, the corpse had to be cremated in a very crude manner. None of the relatives were able to go to this cremation, but out of respect both to the dead child and the worker, I offered to see the thing through. In the dead of night the coffin was taken to an isolated place in the woods, where a hole had been dug and in which a fire was kindled. The coffin containing the dead daughter was laid on this fire, and for me to sit around the fire and watch its progress took all the grace of God I could muster. It was an eerie experience, and one that I do not wish to go through again.

It was strongly suggested to me that since our children had been so close to this little girl who died, they should all be physically examined to determine whether they too might have become contaminated with the disease. Xrays showed that Ruth, our second daughter, was definitely taken by the disease, and Gracie, our youngest, was borderline. There was nothing else to do but rush the family to America. Every ship was filled to the brim, and each steamship company gave us no hope whatsoever for any space for the family for the next few months. Now I was concerned! I had seen this other young lady go down from vibrant health to a corpse in just three months, and how could I bear to see my own daughter go the same way?

"...But God!" I received a telegram from the shipping agents: Thomas Cook & Sons, offering us space immediately, if we were ready to go the next day, as they had just had a cancellation. At the time, my wife was in Arima, but knowing God had undertaken in our serious plight, she went straight to the boat without ever coming home to arrange her personal matters.

While I was rejoicing in this miraculous move of God, the devil began to tease me telling me I would not see Ruth again. Hour after hour he whispered that she would have to be buried at sea, but the devil is a perpetual liar. Not only did she arrive safely in America, but the day their ship arrived, they attended Brother Harry Morris' mission in Oakland, California, and there, at the close of the service, with prayer and the laying on of hands for healing, God touched Ruth's body. Today she is the wife of John Bell, pastor of Revival Temple, and they have two sons, Nathan and David.

But can you imagine my feelings as I stood on the deck of that ship with my family to say good-bye to my wife and three daughters? Our son David continued in Japan with me. War cries were everywhere in the air. A sense of murder prevailed. It was impossible to please the police, and wicked men were using our opposition for their own ends. This on top of my great concern for my daughter with galloping tuberculosis was extremely difficult.

Besides the above problems, the treasury had been scraped to the bottom to get the fares for my wife and daughters. What a situation! But God is the God of all comfort as well as the God of all power. On the very day my family sailed, I received a letter from a Japanese, a former employee of the firm where I had worked many

THE PACIFIC WAR
181

years before. This letter was an apology for having derided my faith in Christ. The man had recently found salvation and felt he owed me an apology for his persecution. What a confirmation that though I had tried to live a Christian life in that office for five years and had seen little results, here, many years later in a time of gross discouragement, the Lord permitted this letter to come at the very time of saying good-bye.

My family headed for San Antonio, and finances were sent from Japan for their upkeep and support. But the Japanese government finally refused to permit this, so a visit to America had to be arranged.

In Japan things went from bad to worse. I began to face the most adverse conditions I had ever known. Foreigners were ordered off the regular foot paths and told to walk in the streets. It was usual for Japanese to spit upon them when they came near, and yet I felt it my duty to continue to give them the good news of a loving Father Who desired their salvation from sin and evil.

Six months later my son David and I arrived in San Antonio. I set up our missionary office in our small house, arranging for our friends to send their offerings there. I knew that I must return to Japan soon, and began to make the necessary arrangements.

Good-byes were said to friends in San Antonio, reservations were made with the steamship company for sailing from Vancouver, and my bags were packed ready to take to the station, when suddenly I felt a peculiar "check" not to go. At first, it seemed like I was weakening, that I might be just afraid of the dangers that I would meet in Japan. I was determined not to be a sissy, and I prayed. Then the Lord showed me this "check" was not due to lack of courage, but was similar to that which God revealed to Paul when he determined to preach in a certain place and the Spirit bade him go elsewhere.

I had allowed myself an extra two weeks both enroute to Canada, and at the port of embarkation for emergencies, so now I decided to delay my departure from San Antonio a

182   IMPOSSIBILITIES BECOME CHALLENGES

week, trusting God to clearly reveal His perfect will for me at that time. Almost exactly to the very time of the first "check," a second check came, and there was now no mistaking that God by His Spirit was leading me to cancel my return to Japan.

One of the longest telegrams I ever sent was soon dispatched to Japan where Sister Dunn and Sister Hughes were still faithfully carrying on in my absence. Arrangements were made for them to go to Hong Kong, and thence to Australia and New Zealand. Had I not obeyed this second check from the Lord, it was evident I would have been on the high seas at the time of the Pearl Harbor bombing, and would have doubtless been caught by the Japanese army.

I learned later that one of the main Japanese newspapers described our work in Ikoma as a camouflage, saying I was not a true missionary but a spy for both the British and American governments. Had I returned to Japan at that time, I would not have been able to do any real spiritual work, but would either have been interned and cruelly treated in prison, or would have been confined to my home unable to purchase food.

How wonderful to know that God moves in mysterious ways His wonders to perform, and how gracious of Him to permit us to detect, to know, and to have the grace to follow these checks and leading of the Spirit!

No sooner had victory been accomplished on this line than another large mountain loomed on the horizon. I have often said that when I gain a victory over what seems an insurmountable obstacle, I feel led to cry out to God: "Give me a greater problem, and a higher mountain." Whether I prayed this way at this time or not, I do not know, but certainly the Lord saw fit to give me one of the greatest mountains I had ever yet faced!

We were in America as visitors, granted a limited time by the immigration laws. We had enjoyed the length granted besides several extensions, but now the law demanded we leave the country. To go to Japan was an utter impossibility; war had just been declared. To take the family over to my native England, was equally impossible. While I had relatives there I had nowhere to go, and no connections in the ministry there. To return to business seemed utterly out of God's will. More than this, our finances hit bottom, and pennies had to be counted when buying groceries for sustenance. There was no possibility of the expensive trip to England.

I cannot express what a tight situation we found ourselves in. For a long time things looked black indeed. At other times a slight gleam of light would appear as there was found a way for myself, as an ordained minister, to stay on in America, as well as my wife and children who were under eighteen. However, our eldest daughter Faith had already turned eighteen and the authorities demanded that she leave the country. Such a situation caused us many sleepless nights. Because of the war conditions the strained financial condition continued, possibly because our friends had been prejudiced by the actions of the Japanese at Pearl Harbor. But faith, praying friends, and earnest crying out to God enabled us to gain another victory through the kindness of the American Consul in Mexico, who lived on this side of the border. With his help and the guarantees of a number of our friends, we were enabled to gain complete victory, and the whole family was granted permission to stay on in America as permanent residents.

REVIVAL TEMPLE

CHAPTER TWENTY SIX

EMMANUEL CHURCH & REVIVAL TEMPLE

*"I will build my Church and the gates of
hell shall not prevail against it."
(Matthew 16:18)*

With a distinct check from the Holy Spirit against my immediate return to Japan, the east wing of the San Antonio Municipal Auditorium was rented every Sunday where friends could gather for worship. I had taken some evangelistic meetings around the country, but possibly due to the prejudice against Japan because of Pearl Harbor, I did not feel that these were particularly successful and felt led to settle down in San Antonio for the time being.

The north side of the city presented a tremendous challenge since there was little Full Gospel work being carried on in this section of the city. Soon a new step of faith was taken in holding services in a much larger building on Josephine street. Later, the purchase of a former Presbyterian church on South Pine street provided a place for the young congregation. This was followed by another step of faith when property on South St. Mary's street was purchased. I had prayed through in my own soul about this latter step, but four or five of the brethren who were serving as an advisory board each shook their heads negatively when looking over the property. Feeling definitely assured of the will of God in the matter, I requested of them the permission to take the step alone, as I was assured God was in it. The next few years proved it to be the will of the Lord, for it was my pleasure to be able to hold the mortgage burning ceremony and preach the last Sunday service in the building a day or so before returning again to Japan.

My son-in-law, John M. Bell, helped me in the early days of Emmanuel Church, as well as Holman Cox and Frank Stribling. Brother Bell has now become the pastor of Emmanuel Church, which took the public name of Revival

EMMANUEL CHURCH & REVIVAL TEMPLE   185

Temple after a new church building was completed on Texas Avenue. The other brethren continued in their own ministries.

It was during the early days of Emmanuel Church that "God and His Bible" radio broadcast was begun, airing every morning seven days a week, and at times twice a day, both in the morning and in the evening.

Looking back to those days brings happy memories of many souls turning to God, some of whom have since entered the glory land, while others are serving their Redeemer faithfully both in Revival Temple and elsewhere. Especially does my heart go back to dear Brother James Phillips, who encouraged me so much in the early days. I can see him now praising the Lord with the tears running down his face, and it was my cherished desire when he passed into higher realms to be at his bedside. God granted me that privilege, and though near the end he was unable to speak, he would pull his hand from under the oxygen tent and point to the sky. Praise the Lord! What a privilege to be permitted to be alone with a warrior of the cross as he entered the pearly gates. His widow, dear Sister Phillips, has since passed on. Brother A. O. Neuman, the first treasurer, has also gone on to his reward.

Another good old soul, dear Sister Robertson, has also gone to her eternal home, and as I write these lines away off in Japan, I realize that at any time I have to face the news of the passing of others.

What wonderful times we have had together in fighting the old enemy when he attacked Mother Williams' body, and what a joy to be able to pray with Sister Boeff when she was in great pain. It is impossible to remember all, but these early days of what was then known as Emmanuel Church, and now Revival Temple, bring back memories of God's divine grace, described as the "unsearchable riches of Christ" in the book of Ephesians.

CHAPTER TWENTY SEVEN

INTERNATIONAL BIBLE COLLEGE

*"Christ ... whom we preach, warning every man, and
teaching every man in all wisdom; that we may
present every man perfect in Christ Jesus.
(Colossians 1:29)*

Many years before the outbreak of the Pacific War there
had been growing within me an awareness of the need for a
definite Missionary Bible and Training College where
missionaries called to Japan could obtain their basic training
in the Word of God, as well as in missionary conditions and
methods of labor. Along with this conviction there had
come a kind of underlying premonition that the Lord might
permit me some time in the future to be connected with
such training, and as I had felt the lack of knowledge of the
Bible among God's people and seen their hunger for a
deeper understanding of the Word, it had come to me that
the time might come when I would spend six months in
Japan as a foreign missionary, and the other six months in
the home field, not only stirring up missionary interest, but
also teaching the Word of God and preparing workers for
the foreign field.

I little realized, however, that God would thus work out
His plan through the upheaval of the Pacific War. Not long
after the outbreak of hostilities it become evident that the
object of opening up a church in San Antonio was a stepping
stone to that of the establishing of a Missionary Bible
Training Institution. The conviction became a deep work of
God. I could not remain satisfied with being a pastor. Prior
to the opening of Emmanuel Church, I had offered myself
to the Lord as a missionary to other fields, and had gone to
quite a deal of trouble and expense in obtaining all the
available literature regarding the many and varied South
American countries.

As night after night I laid myself before the Lord

INTERNATIONAL BIBLE COLLEGE 187

determined to go wherever He led, the conviction grew that I was not to go to another foreign country, but that Japan's doors would open again, and that great and mighty preparations were to be made for a tremendous onslaught into that country at the close of the hostilities.

There was the well meaning opposition from friends because of their limited understanding of the eternal purposes of an unchanging God towards the opening and establishment of another Bible Training College. I can hear some of them say, "But, Brother Coote, do you realize that you are starting a Bible College right from the bottom in a time of great perplexity and in a time of war? It is utterly outside the realm of reason. It cannot be God." Thank God we do not have to be guided by reason in such matters. No matter how reason might agree with the plan, it rested entirely on whether it was the eternal will of God. That is the rule regarding every point. I have proven it to be so through my forty seven years of faith living, and I am determined for the remainder of my life that this shall be the rule. What is the eternal will of God? I am satisfied to know that when I was saved in Japan in the year 1913, He knew of the terrible onslaught of the powers of darkness which precipitated World War II. I am also confident that when the voice of God was heard in the city of Kobe at the close of my five year business contract, "Japan and Pentecost Until Jesus Comes," that our Lord, because of His omniscience, was perfectly informed and knew every detail of the holocausts of the Pacific War. And as I look back today, how thankful I am that He managed matters that we should be a complete family living together in the city of San Antonio, and in spite of many difficulties, trials, and perplexities, how wonderfully faithful He has proven Himself. Hallelujah! Ten thousand times over and over again.

Let me say to any who may still wonder at such a forward move in times of war, if it had not been the will of God, and if the conviction had not been a heavenly one, what in the world could influence me to step out in such a time without any natural resources, while some of our

188   **IMPOSSIBILITIES BECOME CHALLENGES**

friends and supporters were partially influenced against us because of Pearl Harbor? There can only be one answer and that is "it was the eternal purpose of God to establish what is now known as International Bible College." Amen!

Having the assurance that the fact of establishing the school was the eternal will of God, the next two points to decide were the initial finances required for the down payment on the first unit of the buildings required, and the proper location. Thank God we can pray through every detail of such an undertaking, and look back in later years and know that not one misstep was taken. Hallelujah! Scores of available properties were investigated but the leading of the Spirit had not yet been received. 935 West Mistletoe was among these various properties investigated but it was not until some months later, when looking over the property a second time, that there came a distinct witness that this was the place. My word was given and the down payment made. Later years would reveal that 935 West Mistletoe was a marvellous place of blessing, victory, and a jumping off place for the present well equipped campus of International Bible College.

It is impossible in a few pages to go into the many details of the stern fights of faith, miraculous answers to prayer, and the various developments of the college. Brother Frank Stribling, who was the first one to stay in the building, repeatedly said, "Brother Coote, you will never be able to furnish such a building." Little did he realize that not only this building but seven others would be furnished all at the same time as God's will developed for the training of hundreds of young men and women from practically every state in the Union and Canada.

One of the first fights of faith that I can remember was the remodeling of the garage into a class room. A young married believer from San Antonio had been employed to do the work. The necessary materials for the job had been paid for, but the necessary means for the support of this brother's family had not come into my hands by Friday night, and I had promised him faithfully that he would be able to go home and buy groceries for his family by the time

INTERNATIONAL BIBLE COLLEGE

he quit work Saturday noon. I was surprised myself that I had no quivers about the situation, as I knew I did not have a penny Friday night, but God never fails. By the morning's mail a special letter came from a brother who indicated he had a strange, yet definite urge to sell his car and send the proceeds for the school. The offering came right on time and enabled me to pay my brother and meet other urgent obligations.

To relate every circumstance when stark failure faced us and there seemed absolutely no way out of the dilemma, and then see God come across in miraculous ways would take a whole book itself. Well do I remember one noon time telling the students in the dining room that funds had been held up for some reason or other and that there was practically no food or wherewithal to buy any for the next meal. Special prayer was resorted to, and before the time for the preparation of the evening meal a special airmail letter was received from California enclosing sufficient funds to purchase the materials for the next meal. Hundreds of instances of a similar nature made us realize that we were moving in the perfect will of God.

Perhaps this was the reason why one of the outstanding slogans of the college became "IMPOSSIBILITIES BECOME CHALLENGES," the title of the present book. You will notice that the initials of these three words are I.B.C., the initials of the college, as incorporated by Brother William Mulford, a former member of the faculty, and myself, although the college had started under the title of San Antonio Missionary Bible Training College.

In the early days of the college several different slogans came forth, possibly the first one being "I BELONG (to) CHRIST". Another one thought of by one of the students was "INTRODUCING BROTHER COOTE." Each of these had the letters of the institution as the first letter of the word. Still other slogans came into being, some prophetic in nature, such as, "INVADING BIGGER CITIES."

Today graduates and students of International Bible

IMPOSSIBILITIES BECOME CHALLENGES

College fill many pulpits throughout the United States. A number have gone to foreign fields, and many pastors and church workers owe their faith and inspiration to the school. As student after student has said, "You see things happen here, impossible things become realities right before your eyes."

An outstanding event in the history of International Bible College was the acquirement of the new campus. While friends wondered how I would be able to furnish the first building, at 935 W. Mistletoe, the next door building, 915 W. Mistletoe was acquired and became part of the campus, then four other buildings, but the end was not yet. Each of these buildings had been purchased in the direct knowledge of the will of God. It does not mean that there were always funds in hand for the down payment but once God had spoken and made His eternal will and purpose clear, there was nothing else to do but to go ahead.

Naturally, the devil fought every inch of the way, but the Lord never failed. It was clear that one of the buildings should be acquired immediately but there was nothing in hand towards the down payment. Much prayer had been given to the matter and then the Spirit quietly but distinctly made it known to me that I should share my burden with a friend who lived in Chicago. I was not sure that she was able to help whatsoever, but as I waited on the Lord the Spirit clearly showed me that she was to be the one who would make a loan to the school on a business basis. I visited her for this purpose, and quietly stated my case. Would she resent my approach, or had I really been moved by the Spirit of God? Such were the thoughts going through my mind. She also clearly felt it was the will of the Lord to make the loan and a proper business contract was made.

Again I say as I look back, Praise the Lord! He is alive! He is interested in the least detail of the work He has caused us to do, and as He has numbered the very hairs of our heads, so He knows every step of the way. Amen and amen.

INTERNATIONAL BIBLE COLLEGE 191

I must now give the story of the new campus, the present location of International Bible College. I marvel, myself, as I look back and recall the details of this another mighty move of God. I had not any idea that God was going to give us a new campus. Had we not eight buildings already in operation, and were they not sufficient for the work God wished to do through International Bible College? The only hint that God was possibly leading in this direction was the fact that some of the neighbors had complained to the police about the noise of the students praying and praising the Lord, and my wife had felt that if we could possibly get out into the country we could avoid this situation. I had not the least feeling about the matter as we had endeavored to watch the times of praying aloud and praising the Lord so as to not cause any inconvenience to the neighbors.

One day I had quite a headache and felt that I could not continue with the necessary work of the day. Brother Joe Norton, an intimate friend of the work for many years suggested a drive up Fredericksburg Road, as he wished to show me some property. My inward thought was that perhaps my wife had been talking to him about having the campus moved to avoid any more criticism of the neighbors, but not feeling too well I agreed to take the drive, but resented any thought of a new campus for the college.

The property we saw proved to be absolutely inappropriate, and the agent suggested showing us another place. This second property is the present site of International Bible College, composed of ten acres, on a hill overlooking the city of San Antonio. I do not know why, but as I saw it something got hold of my heart. Remember, folks, I did not myself feel the need of a new campus, but the eternal will of God is such that He is greater than our ignorance and even our weaknesses.

In the natural it was utterly ridiculous to give the matter any thought. I did not personally consider the need was an imminent one, and yet the Spirit of God was doubtless working. I amazed myself when I asked for a three to four day option on the property. This was Saturday. Had I

IMPOSSIBILITIES BECOME CHALLENGES

stopped and thought the matter over I would have realized how crazy I was even to do this, since there would be no time to inform our friends or even to ask for their prayerful consideration of the matter.

The following day, Sunday, I asked three of the church folks, those who had lived in San Antonio many years to come and look over the property with a view of receiving their advice as to the location from a property angle. I believe Brother A. O. Neumann was the only man able to do so, and I noticed how quiet he was as he walked across the property and looked into the building which is now known as the administration building. Before getting back into his car, he asked me some pointed questions about the financial indebtedness on the old campus. As I gave him the figures he himself did a little figuring and then said, "Brother Coote, this is of God, go ahead and buy it." I was quite taken aback and must have seemed a little nervous to him when I said, "But Brother Neumann, I do not have a penny in hand, and I only have tomorrow as an option. What shall I do?" Just as if God Himself had come down to earth in human form, I seemed to hear the voice of God speaking to me to go right ahead and give my word for the purchase of the property. From whatever angle I look at the matter now, even after many years have gone by, I am amazed, and consider that if the move was not of God I was absolutely out of my mind, and that there could not be any reason for going ahead and saying, "Yes, I will take the property."

Brother Neumann then asked me to find out what the students themselves could do in making small loans and that he would make the balance necessary to clinch the property. I can see the student body now marching around the main building and shouting the praises of God the next day, for God was in the move, and I can truthfully say it was the quickest and the most instantaneous move that I have ever made in the will of God. Hallelujah!

The deal was closed. The initial payment was made and the property sealed as the campus of International Bible College, because "Impossibilities Become Challenges."

INTERNATIONAL BIBLE COLLEGE

Telephones began to ring, and the occupant of a nearby dwelling did his best to have the contract cancelled. Lawyers were appealed to, and especially the former owner of the property. Though not knowing what he was saying when appealed to, and told by our opposers that he had let the property go to holy rollers, he said, "Well, the only thing you can do about it is to join the holy rollers yourself."

And so a new era in the history of International Bible College began. We were still operating on the old campus, and there were no buildings on the new campus for classrooms, dormitories, etc. but wonderful times were ahead of us. Old army buildings were purchased, torn down, moved to the campus and rebuilt into some of the finest looking buildings any campus could boast of.

INTERNATIONAL BIBLE COLLEGE

CHAPTER TWENTY EIGHT

MISSIONS ON THE MARCH

*"This gospel of the kingdom shall be preached in
all the world for a witness unto all nations:
and then shall the end come."
(Matthew 24:14)*

When Japan surrendered, a conviction came to me that it was time to once again march forward to the regions beyond. It had been for this purpose that International Bible College had been born. The vision for missions had permeated every class and God's heart cry to carry the Gospel to every creature had been the heart of every chapel service.

During the war years we had some evangelistic efforts among the Mexican people of San Antonio, but now the clarion call of "Japan and Pentecost" was heard again. I felt an uneasiness in my spirit for not being among the first of the missionaries entering postwar Japan.

Besides the delay of receiving permits from the American government for entering occupied Japan, another mountain was facing me. I had been fully responsible for the work of International Bible College, ably assisted by my family and the faculty, but the leadership was on my shoulders. It was clearly the will of God to continue training men and women for both the home and foreign fields, and yet, the urgency in my spirit to return to Japan would not go away. I prayed and agonized before the Lord. But days passed without any possible clue of an answer to the problem. I could not possibly be in two places at once. The enemy came accusing me, telling me I had become entangled with the Bible School and financial burdens, and had gotten out of God's divine will.

Reports came from Japan of churches there being crowded and my heart longed to be there to give them the knowledge of Christ. I was not happy. I had to fulfill my

MISSIONS ON THE MARCH

God given call "Japan and Pentecost until Jesus comes." I still had good health and strength, and were not the doors of Japan open as never before? I become restless.

One summer's afternoon, burdened along these lines, I was praying in the upstairs of the administration building when a distinct voice bade me go and see the date of the title deed of the purchase of the new campus. The devil had been teasing me that I had so entangled myself in the work of International Bible College I had forfeited my call to Japan. I knew he was a liar; he always was, and always will be. I went down to the office where the records were kept and to my utter amazement, the purchase of the new campus was on the very anniversary of Pearl Harbor! God said to me, "This is no mistake. I arranged this date to assure you of my will when the devil would try to hinder you. The matter is under my control."

BROTHER COOTE PREACHING AT NARA STATION

CHAPTER TWENTY NINE

MY FLYING VISIT TO JAPAN

"All things work together for good to them that love God, to them who are called according to His purpose."
(Romans 8:28)

Through fifty years of ministry, there have been many impossible situations, but in each case, when I have surrendered everything at my Master's feet, He has always worked out His miracles.

One day while I was working in the International Bible College office, an old friend, Mrs. Pohlman introduced me to a friend of hers named Mrs. Bibby. Immediately our conversation centered around Japan and my burning desire to return. Mrs. Bibby was visiting Texas to sell some property in Dallas owned by her and her sister. I yearned for Japan, yet was blocked by three major problems: the U.S. permit to travel there; funds for the journey; and someone to administer International Bible College in my absence.

Mrs. Bibby challenged me to prayer. She said: "If you pray, and I sell my property in Dallas for my price, I will pay your plane fare to Japan." I began to pray, her property was sold, and I received $1,000 for my return fare to Japan, and her sister, who was converted through all this, sent me another $1,000 for the support of International Bible College. It was not long before the U.S. government granted the permit for me to spend twenty one days in Japan on an investigative trip.

My son, David Coote, seeing the remarkable way God had opened the door for my return to Japan offered to look after the school in my absence. Stopping over in Honolulu on my way, I found Japanese restaurants there, and again realized I was actually a part of Japan.

MY FLYING VISIT TO JAPAN

It is impossible to describe my shock upon arriving in Japan. There was a strange quietness and soberness among the people that comes with deterioration. The taxi ride from the airport to central Tokyo took me through several suburbs that I knew well, and everywhere I was faced with a sense of hopelessness a "shikata ga nai" (it cannot be helped) attitude. There was not a house or shop or any building that did not show signs of degeneration. Windows were broken, fences down, plaster off the walls. It was like a ghost town. Nobody seemed to care enough to do anything about it.

I began to sense the people had suffered a spiritual and mental shock from which it would take years to recover. They had been deceived by their leaders and had all the props knocked from under them, with nothing to take their place.

At the time of the great Yokohama earthquake, it was different. Then, nature had played a game on the nation. This time, they had sacrificed everything in blindly following their leaders, but now had to pay for it by caring for the occupation army. Everything usable was taken from them for living quarters by the occupation forces.

My arrival in Tokyo was on Labor Day. As this was a holiday for officials, it was difficult to find a room. Everything was under the control of the American occupation forces, and I was not allowed to rent a room, buy food, or even ride the trains without official permission. By night I was impressed with the mental anguish on every face. I had heard of inflation but received another shock when I looked over a fruit stand. Before the war persimmons usually priced at around 10 sen each; now they were 10 yen. That was exactly one hundred times higher!

I spent the first two or three days in Tokyo, going hither and thither in my efforts to get a room, have some money cashed, obtaining permits to ride a train to Ikoma where our headquarters were. I had to be fingerprinted over and over, and was sent from one department to another. I cabled my wife: "Conditions unbelievable!" I hardly knew

IMPOSSIBILITIES BECOME CHALLENGES

where to begin. The Japanese, it appeared, had lost heart. There seemed to be no more spirit, no more desire, no more work, and no more ambition. One virtue did seem to remain: I had never seen such patience in my life. The crowds of prewar Japan always jammed the trains and train platforms, but it was a thousand times worse now. The trains were filthy, unkept, and broken down, with no one making any effort to improve things.

Eventually I was permitted to travel to Ikoma, though I was required to stay in a Japanese inn in the city of Nara. I had seen something of the terrible destruction in Tokyo, and in route on the train I braced myself for what I might see in Ikoma. To my astonishment, the buildings were all standing, but all windows were out, and much damage to the walls was apparent. But no bombs had been dropped on the campus. Refugees filled nearly every square foot of the school, and I was immediately faced with the gigantic task of restoring the buildings to continue our God given call, "Japan and Pentecost until Jesus comes!"

My short visit completed, I faced America again, and I cried out to God that I might speak words that would cause many of IBC's young men to give their lives in complete surrender for the preaching of the gospel to the Japanese.

The last leg of the trip back was a stormy one. There was a definite nervousness as I clung to my seat. Minutes passed like hours and the morning seemingly would never come. Thoughts of the ship being torn asunder and I filling a watery grave in the Pacific instead of leading a pioneer band of missionaries to fulfill "Japan and Pentecost" were constantly harassing me.

But we arrived at Los Angeles on time and were told to strap our belts for the landing. The tops of houses could be seen and we expected to begin to feel the bump of the wheels as they touched ground, but we waited and waited, while the plane circled and circled. During the next hour we tried to land again and again but were not permitted, due to heavy fog. There was talk of going to another city, and a second hour passed. I had been told that we only had three

MY FLYING VISIT TO JAPAN 199

hours of surplus gasolene. The stewardess said she had never had such a scary experience before. The third hour went by before faith in the all powerful name of Jesus enabled us to finally touch down.

LEONARD AND DAVID COOTE STANDING IN FRONT OF ONE OF JAPAN'S HUGE IMAGES OF BUDDHA

CHAPTER THIRTY

DIARY OF LEONARD COOTE
THE FIRST WEEK IN JAPAN
SUNDAY, APRIL 9TH TO 16TH, 1950

EASTER SUNDAY, 1950: I can't begin to express my feelings as I awakened this morning knowing we were actually arriving in Japan on Easter Sunday! We had been thrown late by a storm, but the Word of God teaches us that even the wind fulfills His will.

Seeing land again was exciting! No one stayed long at the breakfast table, and by lunch we were docked just outside the breakwater. Passing the medical quarantine was fairly easy; then we took on the pilot and went inside the harbor. Slowly, we drew near the pier, straining our eyes to see if anyone had come to meet us. Someone cried out, "I see three people!"

Imagine our disappointment when we finally got close enough to distinguish faces and learned they were students who were welcoming back one of their teachers. We strained our eyes some more. Where were Jesse Mason and William Nukida? We decided they must have had to be in the Easter services, but after a few minutes, we saw two men running, and Sister Wine cried out, "Look yonder, there are two men and I am sure one of them is a Texan." And to our delight, there were Jesse and William. Brother Wine tried to cry out to them in Japanese "Kansha itashimasu" (Praise the Lord!).

It was a reunion indeed, but we now had to pass immigration. After a great deal of fuss in getting our money exchanged (it is illegal to carry American dollars for more than forty eight hours), we finally got through customs.

We waited for over an hour for a taxi, and as we got in, we had a good laugh over the bag of charcoal setting in the front next to the driver, and learned the reason for this was the car ran on charcoal. We were taken to a hotel so the

DIARY OF LEONARD COOTE

family could rest, as I was to preach in Tokyo that night for Brother Murai.

We received news that ten new students had their bags packed and were ready to come to Ikoma. Knowing there was almost no furniture, beds, tables, or chairs, I knew that I was facing some new mountains upon arrival.

We were unable to stay at any of the European hotels as we had not received permission from the US Occupation Forces, and Sunday being a holiday, we had to go on a Japanese train, traveling all night to Kyoto, thence changing to a tram and a second change at Saidaiji. It was the Wines' first experience at night travel in Japan. The only available food was Japanese food. By six in the morning everyone was glad to get off the train, and I did my best to get some European food for the new missionaries at two of the European hotels, but we were turned down at the first as we had no US permit. At the second hotel special permission was received by telephone and this helped the family a good deal.

After lunch, while waiting for the baggage to arrive in Kyoto I showed them the large temple which is the Buddhist headquarters in Japan. Here we saw six or more large collection boxes. These offering boxes were so large it would take two people to carry them. We also saw the men who were employed night and day to sweep up the offerings thrown to the idols. The sight of men and women, young and old worshipping, cannot but stir your heart, making you aware afresh of the tremendous need for the gospel in Japan!

Since the war, the Buddhists are stirred to greater activity than ever because of the interest Japan is showing in Christianity. Thank God we have something real! Though there are some 250,000 Buddhist priests in Japan who may by their energy try to revive Buddhism, they have nothing to offer for a real experience of sins forgiven.

We gave Sister Wine and the children their first experience of riding in a rickshaw on the way back to the station. At Saidaiji, our changing point, the station master recognized me, and it felt good to know that though I had been away ten years, the impression made upon some of them had lasted, and I trust can be used for their eventual salvation.

Brother and Sister Wine were excited as we walked from the Ikoma station through the marvelous wheat and rice fields, and finally came to the campus of the Ikoma Bible College. They were thrilled, and have since declared it is the most beautiful place in the world. I too feel God has given us a marvelous place for a campus: the purest air, the best water, and tucked far away from civilization, it is quiet and peaceful.

It had been my intention to have Sister Wine and the children stay in a hotel for about a week while I got the Missionary Home ready for them, but the expenses were too high and all of us were out of cash, so we had to pitch in and do what we could to get things in order. Language fails to describe the dirt! The house had not been lived in by Europeans for ten years, but had been used by Japanese refugees who did not know how to keep it. For over a week we scrubbed, washed, and worked hard night and day but felt we had barely got off the first coat of muck and mire.

TUESDAY, APRIL 11th: Hardly had we arrived and gone to work cleaning up the place than we were greeted with shouts of praises as the first bunch of students from Tokyo arrived. What were we going to do? Here they came, shouting the victory, ready to die for Christ just as they were ready to die for their Emperor during the war. One man was to become the boys' dean, and his wife, a splendid woman who worked for General McArthur, was to be my office manager. She spoke English well. Besides them, there were eight young men, all of them splendid young people on fire for God. Though they had traveled all night and had nothing to eat, they were ready to work and get ready for study. When we told them to rest awhile, the first thing they thought about was OPEN AIR SERVICES, and every night this week they have been on the streets, crying out to men and women to repent. How this stirs my soul! I could never have believed this to be in Japan if I had

DIARY OF LEONARD COOTE

not seen it with my own eyes. It is revival indeed!

There were twenty of us in number, including Japanese and Europeans, and here we were without beds or furniture, or bedding, and I feel I could say without exaggeration, practically without anything, but shouting the praises of God and marching to Zion!

The students had their own bedding, but it had not come from the station. They actually slept right on the floor with nothing under them or over them, and it didn't bother them a bit. Some caught colds, but that did not hinder them from marching to Ikoma, a walk of two miles, after another day's hard work to preach the gospel. So far they have not missed a night of street services. They go at it hour after hour, and when they are through, they find anyone who acts interested, take him off to the woods and hold on until he is converted.

I had gone to Kobe to try to locate some second hand beds but their prices were so high, I decided we did not have the money and came back without them. It was hard for us to sleep on hard wooden floors with nothing under us, and little cover, but there was nothing else to do.

Friends in Idaho gave us two sleeping bags. How marvelously God has supplied. We found a rusty old bed on a junk pile, and have given that to the Wine family, and God again is coming to our rescue.

WEDNESDAY, APRIL 12TH: We had to go to Osaka to get permits to buy food, and there we met an old time missionary who told us of someone who had some canvas army cots. He was not sure of their condition, possibly they were broken and some things lost from them, but I took a risk and bought them for $2.00 a piece. When they arrive we will not be sleeping on the floor.

We have not been able to buy plates and saucers. No one has complained, but it is tough going at times. These things are available, but the prices are higher than in America, and all of us arrived with hardly any cash so we must go slow. We now have permits to buy from a government controlled store in Osaka, but besides the high

IMPOSSIBILITIES BECOME CHALLENGES

prices, we must go twenty miles to get it, then pay extra freight, and it arrives several days later. Bread, rice and charcoal are tightly rationed and are nearly impossible to find.

It is hard to describe the poverty and destitute condition of these people, but God is using this to stir them up. I have never seen such hunger for His Word! The people actually grab the tracts out of our hands.

The young men who have come to study in the school are some of the finest you could ever find. They take in every syllable you say, and cannot be stopped from praying, shouting and preaching. I have never seen the like anywhere.

They have come to me without a penny. I dare not eat a bite myself, with such a tremendous on fire for God bunch, and not feed them first. Each one will cost us in the vicinity of $15.00 per month to feed, and with twenty students, that is $300.00 a month just for food. Besides that, I am responsible for feeding the missionaries and providing them with language lessons and living quarters. Already my monthly budget has gone beyond $1,000, but God will provide.

SUNDAY, APRIL 16TH. Today we had our first public worship service. When I saw the people crowding into the Bible School chapel, it was with the greatest difficulty that I kept back my tears. I thought back to our farewell Sunday in San Antonio, but here was the answer to my cries; here was the answer to the beatings I had suffered before the war. Here were Japanese people crowding into the chapel, seeking for a crumb here, a morsel there, or something to satisfy the hunger of their soul.

"Japan and Pentecost" was our slogan, and we had been laughed at because it seemed impossible. But here is a band of men and women, Spirit filled, willing to suffer anything, knowing nothing of laziness, ready to jump when you mention a need, who are the Pauls and apostles of tomorrow. How they sing! How they pray! They are beautiful with hands raised praising the Lord. Many of

DIARY OF LEONARD COOTE

them ragged in dress, some without a square meal in weeks, but they are praising the Lord. I could just weep and weep. This is revival! This is the Word of God being fulfilled. I asked the Lord, Let me teach thousands of them! "This gospel of the kingdom shall be preached into all the world for a witness, and then shall the end come!"

Can you imagine this bunch of young men marching to Ikoma night after night, after working hard, preaching for hours, dealing with sinners until they break through to salvation? Then two or three hours later marching back? No such things as refrigerators. No such things as pop or candy. No such things as the slightest extra in their food. They even apologized when after a week they asked if they could have a little fish with their wheat. See them scraping the leaves off the field in order to save fuel. Look into their eyes and see the glory! This is revival! It is worth sleeping on the floor; it is worth doing without beds; it is worth doing without bread; this is heaven to my soul.

And here they come! Another two new students pleading for entry into the school. Where will it end? I have worked as many as sixteen hours daily since I have been here. Bodies are tired, legs give out with so much walking, but oh what joy in your heart to see their hunger!

I wish I could fly back to International Bible College immediately and bring every member of the senior class to Japan and show them this hunger! I cannot keep still! Tens of thousands of Japanese are milling around looking for a crumb of the spiritual bread of which we have such an abundance! Oh that someone would give me a printing press immediately! One thousand tracts go nowhere. We must print them by the millions. Never before in history has there been such hunger, such golden opportunities!

Dare we be indifferent any longer? In this report I have not done my duty either to you, as those who can pray, give, or come, nor to the thousands and thousands of teeming millions in this land who have been stripped to the bone by their suffering from the war and its resulting surrender, nor to Christ Who gave His all that these hungry souls might get

IMPOSSIBILITIES BECOME CHALLENGES

a glimpse of the marvelous redemption He paid on Calvary's cross.

Though I had not spoken Japanese for ten years, soon after arriving, I had to start with a full schedule teaching the most hungry Bible School students I have ever met! Time and again this week while I was teaching, the whole class stood to their feet and with hands raised they shouted, shouted, and then shouted some more! A few weeks ago, some of these men were Communists; others among them were in a Russian internment camp. The meagerest food, the poorest accommodations, without beds or bedding, eating the lowest form of food, is like heaven on earth to them, because of the power of the Holy Ghost here. I am stirred! And I want you to be stirred, even one thousandth part of what I am! This is revival! This is Japan and Pentecost!

Nothing has been done to get new students. I have not yet sent out the announcement of my return to Japan. My welcome back meeting is not until the following week. We could not possibly have held it before, for there were no benches, no electric lights etc., but this bunch of Spirit filled students do not care about lights, or cups, or plates; they want God, and laugh at you when you talk about lack. They have had a taste of the power of God. They know what Pentecost is, and are not satisfied unless they are in a prayer meeting all the time, praising and shouting hour after hour. This is revival! This is Japan and Pentecost a thousand times over! Hallelujah!

The students came to me today and pled for permission for a FAST DAY tomorrow. I agreed with them that they could only fast breakfast. Their meager daily fare and the long hours they put in for work and study made me feel we should not over do at first.

Now, do you wonder why God has challenged me to plead for fifty missionaries to help us make this revival nationwide? What I have told you about is here in the town of Ikoma, with a population of 10,000. Just twenty minutes away by express tram is the city of Osaka with its three

DIARY OF LEONARD COOTE 207

million souls. I wish to open an EVANGELISTIC CENTER there right away. It is to be a building to hold 300 or more with meetings eight times, every hour of the day. There is also Kyoto in the other direction, about 45 minutes away, with a population of over a million. Then there is Kobe, around an hour away, with a population of one million!

CHAPTER THIRTY ONE

FIRST NEW MISSIONARIES

"Go ye into all the world and preach
the gospel to every creature."
(Mark 16:15)

With the terrible aftermath of World War II, and the desperate spiritual hunger of the Japanese people, the least I could do was to put forth every effort to help bring fifty new missionaries to Japan. Was this not the reason God had led to the establishment of International Bible College in San Antonio?

William Nukida was the first graduate of IBC to come to Japan, followed by Jesse Mason. Brother and Sister Wine and their children arrived with me by ship, and on my next trip over, I was able to bring Mary Harvanka (now Mrs. Abraham Boldt) and Rosella Burnham, both graduates of IBC, also James Alexander, Sister Urie, Abraham Boldt and Clare Carpenter (now Mrs. Jesse Mason). These were followed by Wesley Richert and the Meeks family who took over the work in Fukuoka, Kyushu, started by Brother and Sister Adolph Richert and Brother and Sister Martin Glaeser before the war. Next we were joined by the McKay family, the Jock Wallace family, the Manuel Zamoras, and more graduates of IBC in San Antonio: the Barons, Melugins, Lamar Gillum, Jackie Adams, Marie Hughes, and a former missionary to China, Kathryn Hendricks.

Most of these missionaries spent their first years at the Ikoma Bible College campus either in the missionary home or in one of the various homes built for the convenience of married missionaries while learning the language and the customs. Then they launched out, starting new works in Nagoya, Inuyama, Kashiwabara, Miyazaki Prefecture, Sapporo, Takaoka and other cities. At this writing, some are home on furlough, while Brother and Sister Melugin and Brother and Sister Barron are teaching in the Ikoma

FIRST NEW MISSIONARIES

Bible College.

More than half of the number originally planned have arrived. Now we feel the time has come for another twenty five to come. A Japanese language school is maintained here on the campus, and the missionary home is the receiving home for those just arriving. It is considered absolutely essential that missionaries give their first year in full time language study. We discourage the use of interpreters except for short term special evangelists and visitors.

We do not limit the services of our language school or even the missionary home, but offer both to other missionaries from other missions and groups who strive to make known the riches of God's grace to these teeming millions.

MISSIONARIES IN FRONT OF OFFICE
AND PRINTING BULDINGS

CHAPTER THIRTY TWO

POST-WAR ACTIVITIES

"Always abounding in the work of the Lord."
(1 Corinthians 15:58)

RESTORATION OF BUILDINGS

While reading II Corinthians 2, I became aware that much of our postwar activities were in

"weariness and painfulness"

and

"beside those things that are without, that which cometh upon me daily, the care of all the churches."

Before the war the work was one of developing and enlarging and stepping out by faith into new territories. But now, besides the many details concerning the new missionaries, building small houses for them, arranging their language study, office help etc., there were also the physical buildings of the various churches and the Bible School that needed attention.

It is impossible to describe the condition of these buildings. Today visitors comment on our well kept campus, but it was far different just after the war. "Impossibilities Become Challenges" has been our motto, not only along financial lines, but in every area. The buildings were in such terrible condition, there were actually times when I wished we did not have the campus or the church buildings, so that I could start at scratch and pioneer again. But that was impossible, and the job had to be tackled and endless repairs had to be made.

God's grace has been marvelous through this. Can you imagine having these buildings occupied with unbelievers who in some cases refused to move, as they had nowhere to go? In one case, when after two years in court, we finally found other living quarters for the people and they moved,

POST-WAR ACTIVITIES   211

the building was in such terrible shape, it had to be nearly completely rebuilt.

Over $20,000 was spent in repairs alone. Many trips had to be made to the British Embassy in Tokyo regarding the restoration and registration of the buildings. Even today, we still have one church that is so dilapidated it will cost thousands of dollars to repair, and another church is still occupied by Communist Koreans who challenge the police every time they try to return it to us.

REOPENING OF IKOMA BIBLE COLLEGE

Because of the poor physical condition of the Bible School buildings, I had wanted to wait awhile before reopening the school, but the arrival of many splendid young people forced us to begin classes at once. So I tightened my belt, began to trust God for their support, and began their training. What exciting days these were! Some times I was teaching Japanese to the new missionaries; other times I was teaching the Bible to the new students; and at other times I was on my knees crying out to God for the necessary finances to meet the multiplying obligations. On top of this there were long hours that had to be spent with the carpenter for the repairs. Just when I felt I had gone my limit, here would come another telegram from the government requesting another interview regarding the restoration and registration of the buildings.

SPIRITUAL MINISTRY

But the hunger of the people excited me. The crowds that gathered at the open air meetings inspired me. I had to be at it night and day! We had no car or means of transportation to and from the Ikoma station, and what a drag it was, after standing up in three different trams, being pushed from side to side by the crowds after a long night of heavy evangelism! The body would be totally exhausted.

Have you ever seen a station master with his assistants push and push again an already packed jammed train door, trying to push in more people? This was common, and still is on trains in Japan. If you happened to be inside, you would almost scream because of the pressure. Each night I would ride these trams, changing three times going and coming, and then walk half an hour from the Ikoma station to the school. I literally dragged one foot behind the other, then collapsed on my bed when I reached my home at the top of the hill.

Grumble or fuss at such conditions? No sir! Was I not a missionary, called to give my all, and had I not seen hundreds, literally hundreds of Japanese in the open air meetings with mouths wide open for the gospel? One Sunday I counted 1,200 people standing in the open air just a few yards away from the site where the Osaka Evangelistic Tabernacle stands today.

REACHING THE CHILDREN

CHAPTER THIRTY THREE

OSAKA EVANGELISTIC TABERNACLE

"When He saw the multitudes, He was moved
with compassion on them, because they
fainted and were scattered abroad,
as sheep having no shepherd."
(Matthew 9:36)

My heart has broken many times over the multitudes that can be seen wandering around by the hundreds in the cities of Japan. As mentioned in Chapter Fifteen, just after the great earthquake, I held every night services in a rented building near the prostitution headquarters in Osaka. When we lost our lease after one year, I determined that some day we would own our own property there to carry the gospel to that neighborhood.

God called my attention to some land not far from the very location of the former mission hall, which had been bombed out in the war and was for sale. This was surrounded by small shacks at the time and there was talk that the city might widen the road in the future, which helped to hold down the price of the lot.

The Spirit of God began to move deeply in me with the conviction that He had chosen this place for an aggressive center of evangelism. At this time, Paul Lowenberg visited us, and after seeing the vast crowds that gathered at our open air services on this very lot, he encouraged me to purchase it.

I am not exaggerating in the least when I say this lot was the filthiest, ugliest, most unlikely place for what we wanted. It was actually a dunghill, but I knew God could change things. Finally, after strict investigations were made, the witness came to purchase it. The contract was sealed with a down payment and our friends informed by mail how God was leading.

In addition, the Spirit of God distinctly bade me take an

214 IMPOSSIBILITIES BECOME CHALLENGES

option on the lot next door as well. With trembling hands I signed a contract for the next lot also, and it is on this second lot where we are now trusting God to enable us to erect the basement for the Tabernacle, and later, the main auditorium to accommodate 1,000 people.

With the lot in hand, the next question was the building. Funds were scarce, and we had committed ourselves to purchase and pay for the whole amount of the second lot in a short time. But God never fails! Our attention was drawn to two US army huts that were available and that could be somewhat made into a tabernacle. This was done immediately, and the funds were received by faith and all was paid.

God graciously moved on Brother Lowenberg and the pastor and friends of Life Tabernacle in Shreveport, La., to donate the piano, even before we had any seats. We found some old tent benches, and the dedication service was held. On the first day, three meetings were conducted and seventy new souls knelt at the altar and gave their lives to the true God, the Lord Jesus Christ!

Revival came, and every night the altars of the tabernacle filled up. Hot weather did not hinder a bit. God greatly used Brother James Alexander with his beautiful piano playing, and as we saw souls saved night after night, we knew that God had definitely led us to the right spot for a revival center in the middle of the most active, sinful area of Osaka, a city of three million souls!

An illustrated Japanese magazine sent their photographers and published articles about the new work; city papers wrote up favorably. One seminary sent their students to learn how to do evangelistic work. The believers graciously yielded to our teaching about giving, and the temporary tent benches were replaced by permanent ones bought by the new believers. One year passed without a single night off. The second year continued with services every night, and we now celebrate our third year of continuous operation with the doors opened every night. That means 1,000 nights of dynamic evangelism. Praise the

OSAKA EVANGELISTIC TABERNACLE

Lord!

During the first year of the tabernacle, a children's evangelistic service was held every Sunday afternoon, and as many as 400 children would crowd into the building. These children were then divided into classes according to their ages and given more detailed teaching, each having his own New Testament. This gradually developed into a morning Sunday School much like our Sunday Schools in America. But soon we were out of space. At this time there were no toilets, no running water, no place for a watchman to stay, no room for offices, no prayer room, and everything was jammed with people.

Another step of faith brought the tabernacle annex into being. Plans were drawn, and the new believers assisted with the work. God graciously moved during a Missionary Convention at Revival Temple in San Antonio, and they sent two thousand dollars just at the time when we had come to the end of our resources in this new project. But Jesus never fails!

Often the tears have rolled down my face as I have witnessed a house full of Sunday School children, each with his testament pressed to his bosom, singing with all their hearts "Into my heart!" It grips me friends! Something grips my whole being, as we are located in a district where the need is the greatest, where there are few, if any other churches or Christian homes. My heart cannot rest until I have accommodations for 1,000 children and the various rooms and equipment to train them to be true Bible Christians!

On Tuesday nights our Sunday School superintendent, Miss Komiyama, trains the new Christians to be teachers and workers. We hope to have a kindergarten in connection with the tabernacle shortly.

Page after page could be written of this wonderful tabernacle! Every one who comes over to minister here speaks of the marvelous spirit and tremendous opportunity here! Brother Morris Plotts; my son David Coote of IBC; my son-in-law, John Bell, of Revival Temple in San

IMPOSSIBILITIES BECOME CHALLENGES

Antonio; my daughter, Grace Cathcart who thrilled the people with her trumpet playing; and Brother Batke of the Apostolic Church of Pentecost in Canada, all were excited about the work.

What has stirred me is knowing there are converts from the tabernacle to be found all over Japan: in various other Bible Schools, and as workers with other missionaries. In the city of Nara, a whole family who was saved at the tabernacle, became the nucleus for a church. In Amagasaki, there is now a new church forming as a branch from the tabernacle. The head of a factory dormitory was converted and became the leader in this branch church. Their average in Sunday School for the past two months has been 230 children.

Our morning worship services at the Osaka Evangelistic Tabernacle are times of great blessing. Most of the believers are now filled with the Spirit, and various gifts of the Spirit are being manifested. Four solid Christian men converts of the Tabernacle have been chosen as elders, and they are proving to be wonderful leaders for the work.

This record of the beginnings of the Osaka Evangelistic Tabernacle is given here to encourage you to go ahead with what you know to be the will of God, in spite of all opposition, unbelief, or seeming impossibilities.

A host of difficulties and terrible obstacles met me when we began with the building of the larger auditorium known among us today as the New Wing. The first wing was supposed to only last one year, though we have used it for fourteen years. The time will come when it will be condemned, torn down, and an extension of the New Wing will be added, to the consternation of the forces of hell, for this is a positive lighthouse to the mighty power of the gospel of Jesus Christ! Though its doors have been open for fourteen years with services, large or small, being held every night, it is now being considered to take off on Monday nights, so we can begin extensive evangelism in other areas.

At this writing, the New Wing has been fully completed downstairs, with faith being exercised for the second story.

OSAKA EVANGELISTIC TABERNACLE 217

Literally thousands of souls constantly come through its doors and find the Lord.

On the outside, the New Wing appears like an up to date bank building, and inside it has a splendid auditorium. Its location is without doubt, the very best fishing place in all of Japan. It has a full size altar running from east to west, and at the close of our Friday services, this altar is filled with pastors of our mission seeking God for the lost. The altar is always full at the close of the service, and untold thousands have found the Lord here.

OLD AND NEW OSAKA EVANGELISTIC TABERNACLE AT NIGHT

CHAPTER THIRTY FOUR

ESTHER COOTE'S CORONATION

*"Who can find a virtuous woman? For
her price is above rubies."
(Proverbs 31:10)*

It was noon and I had just finished talking with two pastors in my office and was walking back to my apartment when a telegraph boy handed me a cable. On opening it, I was stunned by the news of Esther's death! I said nothing to the two pastors who were walking with me, but continued to my home, and prostrated myself before the Lord, committing it into His hands.

What was I to do? In a few minutes the two pastors knocked at my door. They did not know the contents of the cable but from the change they saw on my face, they knew something serious had happened. Slowly, I explained it to them, and to my surprise, they both fell prostrate on the floor weeping!

This was Friday, and that night was the weekly fellowship service at the Osaka Evangelistic Tabernacle with our pastors and Bible School students. Should I not get in touch with my children in Texas? I decided to go to the Tabernacle and afterwards try to telephone Texas from a hotel in Osaka.

The next day word came that the telephone operator was searching for me, and after considerable waiting at the telephone office, I finally heard David, my son's voice.

David had contacted many friends and pastors in America who had graciously enabled him to cable my return fare by Pan American Airways. With almost no preparation, I flew the next day via Los Angeles, where I was met by Pastor David Schoch and Charles Hardin. I went on to San Antonio, arriving early the next morning.

What a sight met me as I left the plane! All four

ESTHER COOTE'S CORONATION 219

children and their families: Faith, David, Ruth and Grace, standing in the gateway! They later told me that when I met them, the keen edge of the awful shock of their mother's sudden death had been tempered somewhat by my coming.

As a family, God had brought us through many disasters: the great Yokohama earthquake, the loss of Mary Anna, the tremendous persecution before the war, our separation when Ruth was struck with galloping tuberculosis, and World War II. I experienced a tremendous surge of praise and worship to our blessed Savior as I placed my arms around each one. And when we went to the funeral home and together looked into the sweet face of darling Esther, we declared: "She is not here, but she is safe in the arms of Jesus. She has fought a good fight and is now entered into her reward."

How many battles of faith we had fought together, bringing into being the Ikoma Bible College, the Osaka Evangelistic Tabernacle, a number of smaller churches in Japan, and the Taejon Bible College in Korea, and International Bible College and Revival Temple in San Antonio!

Esther's funeral service will never be forgotten, especially the graveside committal. I could not help it, but raising my hands I praised the Lord, even speaking with other tongues. The funeral director thought I was speaking Japanese, but no, it was my spirit rejoicing for God's faithfulness to us together through the years! It was Esther Coote's coronation.

Is not our God faithful, and His promises true forever? No preparations for the sudden departure of my beloved wife had been made, but within twentyfour hours of her funeral, I was able to declare that all expenses for the funeral, the lot and my return fare to Japan had been fully met and settled!

Praise God from Whom all blessings flow;
Praise Him all creatures here below;
Praise Him above, ye heavenly host;
Praise Father, Son and Holy Ghost! Amen.

ESTHER COOTE

CHAPTER THIRTY FIVE

SOUTH KOREAN BIBLE COLLEGE

"Teaching every man in all wisdom."
(Colossians 1:27)

It had been with great reluctance that I had surrendered to the idea of building a third Bible College in South Korea. Many of our Korean converts from pre-war Japan had returned to their native land and they were pleading with me to do in Korea what God had enabled to be done in Japan. I must confess that I felt I had done my duty with building two Bible Colleges already, and now to be challenged with a third, seemed a bit too much. Also, Korea was war stricken, and its improper sanitation and lack of food was a real threat to health.

"Where duty calls or danger, be never wanting there" was a phrase that came often to my spirit. Finally, God's will was confirmed and I made several trips by sea to investigate property and try to find the right location. In building our Bible Schools I have stayed away from the capitals because often theological institutions are located there and this appeals to the pride of man. Instead, I look for a place with a good railway or other transportation just outside the city limits in the country.

In Korea, difficulties met me as usual, with problems and dangers galore. I even had to deal with deception by false brethren. On one occasion I decided upon a certain property and paid down the first payment, and a month later when I returned to Korea to pay the balance, the so called Christian who had dealt with me, had sold the same property over my head to someone else.

"Many are the afflictions of the righteous, but the Lord delivereth him out of them all."

Thank God He finally led us to the present ground, and I was introduced to one of the finest Christian gentlemen, an elder in a Presbyterian church, who was an experienced contractor. This brother has exercised great patience with me in the erection of the twelve buildings there which include men and women's dormitories, class rooms, native workers' homes, a fine chapel and two European style homes for missionaries.

Many times when I was unable to meet the payments, he showed the most wonderful patience; in fact he never came to see me without first praying God's blessing on my little cottage.

What glorious times we have already seen in Korea! Many scores of young men have graduated from our Bible College there and are gone forth into the rich harvest fields of Korea! Wonderful evangelistic campaigns have been held with many Korean pastors, originally converted and filled with the Holy Ghost in our work in Japan, who have come from all parts of South Korea for fellowship and encouragement.

CHAPTER THIRTY SIX

TAEJON (KOREA) EVANGELISTIC TABERNACLE

"EVERY CREATURE"

Again it would be impossible to give an accurate account of the endless difficulties I faced for the erection of the Taejon Evangelistic Tabernacle.

During my conversion experience, soon after my first arrival in Japan, I was greatly influenced by men like J. B. Thornton, Barclay Buxton, Argall, Paget Wilkes and many others. I was convicted that salvation was not merely a personal experience, but its purpose was that I must embrace the whole world and every person in it, and help them to know the gospel of the Lord Jesus.

I was not to be a missionary to all the foreign lands, but I was responsible to give, to pray, and to interest myself in every country. While still in business, I walked several blocks each day to my office from the interurban train. With my eyes open I would pray for the unsaved, the missionaries, and the native pastors around the world.

I used the letters of the English alphabet to guide me in covering as many fields as possible. The first day I took the letter "A" and Africa was brought to mind. The next day it was "B", and though I knew very little of Bechuanaland, I believed that I could pray effectively in the Spirit, even with my eyes open and walking down the street, for the works of God in that land.

Was it any wonder then, that after the various buildings were built and paid for at the Taejon Bible College, that my heart went out to these poor, war stricken Koreans who had never had the opportunity of knowing about the Pentecostal baptism of the Spirit as revealed in Acts 2?

My heart cry must ever be Onward! Onward! In the full revelation of the will of God. Daily in Taejon I took my exercise walking through the streets of the city. Yes, like the spies investigating the city of Jericho, I was on the move again. Two or three times I found a likely spot for the Taejon Evangelistic Tabernacle, only to be informed that it was already sold.

Finally God gave the witness to the selected site. I was able to pay for the land in cash, singing hallelujah, and next face the bigger task of the building. The following New Year my son David came to Japan as the New Year's convention speaker, and while there we came to Korea to show him the new land. He felt it was too small, in view of the fact this may be the first Pentecostal church in the city, but it was a good start, even on a smaller basis, and later we can build again, maybe twice its size.

We have just graduated eight of the finest Korean men and women from the Taejon Bible College and seven of them are going into direct evangelistic work, mainly in places in and around Taejon, so that my vision of a ring of smaller churches in and around the city will be fulfilled.

I am determined to fill this city with the news of Pentecost. I am determined to see one of the greatest outpourings of the Spirit in this city!

TAEJON EVANGELISTIC TABERNACLE

CHAPTER THIRTY SEVEN

THE PHILIPPINES - MY FOURTH BIBLE COLLEGE

"My thoughts are not your thoughts, neither are
your ways my ways, saith the Lord."
(Isaiah 55:8)

Who would ever have thought it? While I was celebrating my 74th birthday, the frequent requests of Brother Eugene Garrett of the Philippines began to move in the depths of my soul. Ever determined to only move in the full will of God, I was inclined to shelve the request. But when Brother Garrett invited me to come over for his monthly workers' meeting, I felt impelled to go and to explore the matter of a Bible College for his workers. About this time I received an offering earmarked for the Philippines. Things seemed to be taking shape.

I made certain suggestions to Brother Garrett and also wrote a monthly bulletin for his workers, offering to undertake a short term course of about two months yearly at the beginning. I also offered, as God provided, to give the month of January to teaching in the Philippines as much as five or six hours a day.

Brother Garrett has the Bible College ground bought, paid for, and registered. The believers and workers are giving of their means for the erection of the simple buildings to house the students while the school is in session.

What a privilege to know the will of God! What joy it is to be led of His Spirit and to minister His Word to those called of Him who are willing to sacrifice and plunge into the jungles where there are absolutely no conveniences whatsoever, and bring into being many gospel chapels for the full truth of the Pentecostal message of the Lord Jesus Christ!

CHAPTER THIRTY EIGHT
(An Appendage)

BREAKING FORTH ON THE RIGHT HAND
AND ON THE LEFT

"For thou shalt break forth on the right hand and on the left; and thy seed shall inherit the gentiles and make the desolate cities to be inhabited."
(Isaiah 54:3)

As with Abel, who "being dead yet speaketh," so Leonard Coote's vision and ministry live on through the lives of those he impacted. On February 23, 1969, he went home to be with the Lord Whom he dearly loved. His new wife, Frances, whom he married on January 4, 1968, in the home of his daughter Faith in Dallas, Texas, faithfully cared for him during his last months of illness in San Antonio.

The works in Japan, Korea, and San Antonio that he founded continued to grow: the Japan ministry was led for several years by David and Lana Copp of Long Beach, California; the work in Korea was led by David and Judy Merwin and later by Gary and Beverly Pokorney, both of whom were graduates of IBC in San Antonio; and the work in San Antonio continued under his son David Coote over International Bible College, and his son-in-law, John Bell over Revival Temple.

In 1978 Revival Temple built and dedicated a lovely new sanctuary where they are still seeing the excitement of a full house and a constant fresh flow of revival and a foreign missionary outreach to many countries.

In 1984/85 David Coote built and dedicated a beautiful large facility to accommodate the various activities of International Bible College. Thus the vision given to Leonard Coote many years ago continues to be fulfilled through the lives of young people trained at IBC under David and Hope Coote and the team of teachers God has

BREAKING FORTH 227

given them. At the time of this writing, over one hundred graduates of IBC have gone forth to various mission fields of the world, besides many who are working in America as pastors and in church related ministries. Altogether over 2500 students have attended International Bible College.

Today, the year 1990, the work in Japan continues to expand. Leonard Coote's grandson, John Cathcart and his wife Gloria, both graduates of IBC, are missionaries in Japan where John has already built a lovely church in the city of Tenri - home of a strong strain of Buddhism called Tenrikyo - and a city so wholly given to idolatry, no Christian work has ever succeeded in the past. John's church is mostly young people and young couples, and they have a dynamic vision to reach five surrounding areas, and have been praying for five missionary couples who will go into these towns and start churches. At this writing, four of these five areas have already been started.

John Cathcart is the son of Leonard Coote's youngest daughter Grace Hearn, who resides in Plano, Texas, with her husband Raymond. John's wife Gloria is the daughter of Pastors Delmar and Juanita Hyman, former missionaries to Africa. Gracie's oldest son, Rocky, is a medical doctor.

The Bible College in Ikoma, Japan is presently preparing to rebuild many of its buildings to accommodate its growing Japanese student body, and is under the leadership of Pastor Yoshiyuki Sakae, pastor of the church in Tomio, who was trained under Leonard Coote in the fifties and sixties. Pastor Sakae's older brother, Ikko Sakae is the current pastor of the Osaka Evangelistic Tabernacle, faithfully carrying out the vision for which the Tabernacle was established by Leonard Coote.

Faith Denton, Leonard Coote's oldest daughter, resides in Dallas, Texas, where her daughter and son-in-law, Sam and Daphne Eaton, pastor Life Temple. This church was founded by Faith's late husband, Wally Denton, who also spent several years as a missionary in Japan with Brother Coote before World War II. Their son, David Denton and his wife Jerrie, pastor a church in Dumas, Texas, and their

IMPOSSIBILITIES BECOME CHALLENGES

youngest daughter, Debbie, with her husband, Mark Wallis, share in the ministry of the Dallas church.

David and Hope Coote had three children: Timothy Leonard, who went to be with the Lord in July of 1990; Rebekah Ruth, married to Van Pinner Jr., a naval reserve and airline pilot, and Anna Joy, married to Troy Parker, a pastor in Crowley, Louisiana.

Ruth Bell, Leonard Coote's third living child, is the wife of Pastor John Bell of Revival Temple in San Antonio. They have two sons: John Nathan, a commercial builder, and David Michael, who is Associate Pastor and Minister of Music at Revival Temple.

Just before Leonard Coote went home to be with the Lord at their humble cottage at 214 Colfax Street in San Antonio, his daughter Ruth asked him if he had a word for the Missionary Board which was meeting at that time. With his weakened voice, and struggling to get the word out, he whispered, "Yes, FORWARD!"

This has ever been the vision and watchword of Leonard Coote, pioneer missionary to Japan. The tent stakes have been strengthened through his family and ministries that he trained, making it possible for the cords to be lengthened, reaching out through pastors and missionaries circling the globe and proclaiming the good news to those who have never heard. Truly, his life and ministry have broken forth on the right hand and on the left, and his seed is making the desolate cities to be inhabited with the gospel!

LAST COOTE FAMILY PICTURE TAKEN IN 1962

BACK ROW (Lefft to right): Timothy Coote, Walter Denton, John Bell, David Coote, David Denton, Dapne (Denton) Eaton, David Bell.

CENTER ROW (Left to right): Faith (Coote) Denton, Ruth (Coote)Bell, Leonard Coote, Grace (Coote) Hearn, Hope (Schrader) Coote.

FRONT ROW (Left to right): Becky (Coote) Pinner, Anna Joy (Coote) Parker, Debbie (Denton) Wallis, John Cathcart, Rocky Cathcart. Nathan Bell not in picture.